A GREENHORN GAL:
LIFE IN EASTERN
MONTANA

Best wishes
from a greenhorn gal!
Virginia A. Johnson

Best wishes!

From a grandson Ted!

Virginia K. Johnson

A GREENHORN GAL:
LIFE IN EASTERN MONTANA

Virginia A. Johnson

ISBN: 0692896074
ISBN 13: 9780692896075

Contact **Virginia A. Johnson** at:
vajwriteup@q.com

In Remembrance
Dave Lassle
1953-2017

Contents

Acknowledgements

I thank my husband, Wayne, for his help and encouragement during the process of writing this book. Without his prodding, "A Greenhorn Gal: Life in Eastern Montana" would be little more than a pile of manila folders filled with notes.

My gratitude goes to cousins Shirley and Lillie, and Kathy Galland, co-owner of Prairie Unique, in Terry, Montana. These three women took time to read parts of the manuscript and gave me, a genuine greenhorn gal, their constructive comments. A special thanks goes to my former editor, Steve Lundeberg. He agreed to do a major edit of my quirky little book.

My three children, Sharon, Lynn and Andrew, are my quiet cheerleaders. You have my love. To my daughter-in-law, Tori, and my son-in-law, Ron, thank you for being caring and supportive. To my five grandchildren, Jasmine, Kerryn, Kyah, Teague and Keane—may each of you learn the joy of writing stories.

Introduction

Although born and raised in Portland, Oregon, my roots to the state of Montana go back over a century.

In 1763, Catherine the Great, ruler over the entire empire now called Old Russia, issued a manifesto. This document encouraged foreigners, specifically German farmers, to immigrate to Russia, settle there and produce food from her vast, fertile lands. Ancestors of my maternal grandparents, Joseph and Christina Hettich Gaub, responded to the czarina's invitation.

Records reveal these ancestors traveled from what is now southern Germany to the area now designated as the country of Moldova around 1805 and settled within the old Glückstal Colonies then located in the region north of the Black Sea.

Joseph and Christina, young adults with two small children, sold their property in Russia, boarded ship and sailed to America in 1901. Several close family members accompanied them on the voyage. After passing rigid entry requirements at Ellis Island, they bought land near Bowdle, South Dakota. Around 1911, my grandparents uprooted their growing family one last time. They resettled in eastern Montana, purchasing land on the banks of Cabin Creek, east of the little town of Fallon.

My mother, Anna Marie Gaub, was the sixth of the couple's nine living children. Born in 1909 and raised between her two beloved brothers, Joseph and Henry, Anna grew up with a deep desire for learning beyond the eighth grade, and to see the world, two yearnings not approved by her devout and strict Protestant parents. After graduation from high school and then nurse's training, Anna, like tumbleweed driven by unpredictable winds, meandered her way westward to Portland, Oregon.

She married my father, Clifford (Perkins) Renoud, in Portland, on February 21, 1940. They lived most of their 47 years of married life in the northeast part of outer Portland, in an old 1909 farmhouse built on two acres of woodland. The couple had two children, my older brother, Winston, and me. During our growing up years, we made two road trips to Fallon to visit Mom's relatives. In 1981 my family, accompanied by Winston's family and our now elderly parents drove to Fallon. It proved to be my father's last trip east.

After my father's death, Mom and I flew to Montana four times, from 1988 to 1997. Each visit there, my first cousin, Shirley, Uncle Henry's only child, would encourage me to purchase one of the old, abandoned homes in Fallon. After some contemplation of the idea, and a good deal of prayer, that is exactly what my husband, Wayne, and I did. We purchased a dilapidated old house in the summer of 1998. Mom's older sister Christina and her husband, Christ Schock, lived at this site decades earlier. When we came to our senses, Wayne and I realized Christina's place would not be livable. But in 2001, a small home came up for sale just down the road and we snapped it up. We now live at this home in Fallon two months a year, May and September. What keeps us coming back to this dry, seemingly barren region again and again? We drive 1,200 miles one way for two things: the people and the landscape.

We cherish the times spent with the relatives I rarely saw growing up. Time runs out for all of us. Aunts and uncles, along with several cousins, have passed from this life during our years spent in Montana. Then there are the folks we have met, and the friends we have made during our stays. Treasures each. Montana's landscape is a great treasure, too. Be it the high peaks of the Rocky Mountains, the flatlands of farming, or from the western forests to the harsh, sparse geography edging the Badlands, the state is almost too big, too diverse to mentally grasp. It is even more so when one drives through it during seasonal changes.

Virginia A. Johnson

Each spring we marvel at how Montana, locked deep within winter, begins to unfurl evidence of becoming fruitful again: budding trees, wildflowers in bloom and rivers like the Clark Fork and the Yellowstone running high with melted snow. On our September visit, chill comes about mid-month, with the cottonwoods beginning to change color, and the shrubs in the ravines and coulees putting on their red and purple coats. For me, trying to absorb it all became almost overwhelming, so I started putting to paper what I saw and heard, what I smelled and tasted. Early on I fashioned little stories from these notes. After having a few of them published in regional periodicals, I stood what I'd written on end, added more to it and then realized there might be a little book trying to find its feet.

In "A Greenhorn Gal: Life in Eastern Montana" the reader will discover some short stories that are whimsical, others that are biographical and one or two of a more thoughtful nature. I included a section on recipes, each one introduced by a story, because recipes are insightful concerning the peoples of a particular region and therefore part of the historical narrative. Most important, I wrote this book with the idea that a reader could open it, read a story or peruse a recipe, put the book down, and then come back to it another time. I encourage you to take each story as a tale from the eyes and senses of a greenhorn gal, and may you relish your read.

Part I

The Nut Bucket

After we purchased our home in Fallon, and during our trip east in May 2003, I discovered the purpose of cattle branding. Boy, did I ever. Methods of branding have changed since that day a number of years ago, but I will never forget my initiation to this rite of passage for young bulls.

"You can carry the nut bucket," said Dani, my cousin's then 10-year-old granddaughter. It was the day before her family's annual branding. "I had to carry it last year but I found some other kid and got rid of it." With that, she dashed off to somewhere else.

Nut bucket? Now what did she mean by that?

As a kid growing up in Portland, Oregon, I used to collect walnuts in late fall, plunking them into a paper bag or small pail. Is that what she meant?

Or maybe she was talking about the kick-about bucket most households have, the receptacle for loose nuts, bolts and nails. Why would I need to carry that around at a branding?

Branding. Nut bucket. Small innocent bulls.

Innocent bulls soon to be sad little steers.

Yes, it looked like I would get it all right.

This was the second year to attend my eastern Montana relatives' annual spring brandings. True, I attended one when I was an 8-year-old city kid, but that does not count. Back then I was young enough to get away with riding my cousin's gentle horse, Trixie, around in a circle and well away from all the bawling, burning and whatever other nasty stuff might be going on. Not anymore.

The previous year, at my first branding in about 45 years, I disgraced myself. One look at the swirling horses, protesting cows and people running about with hot pokers and such, I did what any city woman would do. I hid behind the outer fence and watched it all through the slats. For hours. When nature called, I hunted up a forlorn bush — they don't call this the Badlands for nothing — never forgetting I was in rattlesnake country, that cowboys had good long-distance vision, and that there are few white-faced cattle in these parts. Afterward, I vowed that the following year I would be more…prepared.

I came to the next branding with a lawn chair. My 35mm camera was loaded with film, while my bladder arrived empty. With scuffed Nikes and faded Gap jeans, I should fit in. After all, I am a retired teacher. My place is as a detached observer. I'll just watch my husband, Fly Tag Boy, while he does his thing.

And then I made my first mistake. This curious woman moseyed inside the corral.

"Virginia, could you tally for me?" It was Darren, Dani's father, and he looked harried. More than a hundred restive calves and their upset mamas milled around us. He proceeded to draw a series of what looked like hieroglyphics on a page in a small notebook. Darren quickly explained each brand. "Keep count of which heifers and which bulls have which of these brands," he added.

Bar XY...bulls...Heart Lazy T...heifers...O Bar 4.

Anxiety, like one of those resident rattlers, uncoiled from my stomach and slid its way up my throat. Could I keep it straight? I *should* be able to do this, I told myself. Didn't I have a college degree? Hadn't I taught school? Laboriously, I rewrote Darren's scratchings to a more readable form. A part of my brain wondered how Dani's father had fared in penmanship at school. But right now, his faulty handwriting was the least of my worries.

Then it dawned on me. To know the heifers from the bulls meant I had to be right up front and personal when the cowboys did the big C word to those poor little guys. I had to keep one eyeball on the branding, and one eyeball on the other task at hand.

I started to protest, but then realized the other option: I would end up with the nut bucket. I clutched that little notebook and that pencil like my life depended on it. Bring 'em on!

Kabam! In came the calves, three and four at a time. Down went the critters. Swoosh came the branding crews. In 30 to 45 seconds, each calf was ear-tagged, inoculated, branded and when applicable, relieved of his bullhood.

I hippity-hopped around trying to do my job without getting run over by men on horses, trampled by upset cows or accidentally vaccinated against Black Leg, BVD, and Red Nose.

I could not keep up. All that smoke and those bodies in the way. I could not see to do my job. The smell of burning hide, the sight of the bloody, sloshing nut bucket, and the sound of calves' pitiful cries made my stomach turn.

"I don't think I will be interested in eating afterward," I said to no one in particular. I have been known to say off-the-wall stuff when in deep distress.

"Aw, your appetite will come back," someone replied.

This was even worse than the year we took all the fourth-graders at our school on a two-day field trip to central Oregon. This was the trip where the kids started vomiting all over the inside of the school bus, and I had diarrhea. The one I later called The Field Trip From Hades.

I prayed for help. It came in the form of a teenage girl brandishing a hypodermic needle the size of a turkey baster.

"Could you help me?" I pleaded. I explained my problem.

It did not take long for that bright young woman to assess the situation. She found her kid brother and hauled him over to me.

"Here," she said, "Charles can help you." Charles looked like a nice, intelligent kid. He did not smile. The teacher part of me rose to the surface.

"Charles, we will work counterclockwise. Start there." I pointed to a calf, already down and being worked on like a piece of raw meat besieged by hornets. "I will be off to the side. You tell me the brand and if it's a boy or a girl." He looked at me, nodding but saying nothing. Courteous child, I thought. Listens when his elders speak.

Charles proved to be nice, bright, polite and also quick. He kept ahead of it all. Even with a can of pop in one hand.

Tally Girl stayed right with him. In fact, when all was said and done, we were only one off on our count. Better yet, I managed to keep one foot ahead of that nut bucket.

At dinner later on, right there near the corral and my plate heaped full, I had a chance to reflect. This is the educator's way of saying I hunkered down and did some thinking. Brandings aren't that awful. A branding protects both the herd and its value to the owner. This spring ritual gives people a chance to help each other, and to visit after a long, cold winter. The teenage girl with the hypo plans to be a veterinarian. Whether she ends up a vet or not, what a valuable experience for her!

And me? I learned several things.

I learned how to read a brand. The contents of the nut bucket, as one seasoned calf wrestler assured me, "are the best source of protein there is." My Nikes survived cow poop and blood splatter. A person becomes accustomed, sort of, to the sights, sounds and smells at a branding. I proved I could be Tally Girl but with help. Most important, I liked my title. It beat being called Nut Bucket Woman, that's for sure.

Spring Branding

Quilt Hop Quest

Our Honda CRV roared up the side street of a small town in Montana. I snuck a peek at my watch. Aha! The place would still be open. If lucky, I would hit pay dirt. The driver of the rig, my husband and co-conspirator, knew the exact location of the old bank. He pulled the overheated vehicle to the closest parking space.

I leaped out of the car and bolted toward the building. As I approached the bank, several women slid out the massive front door, smiles on their faces and arms loaded with loot.

I pushed past them with barely a nod. Stay focused, I told myself, no fishy-fancy chatter until the mission is accomplished. Clutched to my bosom were the two things essential to carrying out this deadly earnest task: my quilt hop passport and my Visa.

There is nothing more important to serious quilting addicts than a quilt hop quest organized by fabric stores. Women have been known to exceed the speed limit, not stop for lunch and max out credit cards while on such an adventure.

For those who have no idea but are a wee bit curious, read on.

A quilt hop is not a bunch of women, quilts draped over their shoulders, white socks on their tootsies, dancing to 1950s music.

A quilt hop, sometimes called a quilt safari or quilt rendezvous or whatever crazy theme is cooked up during the bottom days of a Montana winter or the sizzling heat of summer, is a contest sponsored by a group of fabric stores. It happens within a short period of time, usually no longer than two weeks. The goal for quilters is to visit each shop, have their personal passport stamped, purchase fabric and then head down the road to the next store. The completed passport often becomes the ticket to win some really luscious prizes. A store listed on the designated map might also hold a drawing for goodies, or reward those who stop by with a small gift. Sometimes the rules change as the years go on, or the economy falls head first into a well, but the goal is the same: Get people into those fabric stores. Buy! Buy! Buy!

In Montana, participating shops are often spread far apart from each other. For instance, if the first store is east of Missoula and the last one is near Wolf Point, or even into North Dakota, this means putting a load of miles on a rig, and in a hurry.

So who cares about these safaris, etc.? Herds of quilters, owners of fabric stores and the Montana Highway Patrol, that's who.

Quilt hops, usually held in the spring and again in the fall, mean more to quilters than zooming from store to store in hopes of winning prizes. They let fellow addicts know they're still alive after the frigid winter or scorching summer and provide a chance to meet new people while ogling the fabulous quilts each store displays as eye candy. Along the route, everyone learns what latest patterns are hot, and what are not — most important as quilters view bolts of gorgeous, sensuous, addictive fabric, all seemingly must-haves to survive the coming whatever. To the hooked, the new fabrics, patterns and do-dads really are worth blowing a serious chunk of change. In simple terms for quilters, it's money out.

The owners of fabric stores are a shrewd bunch. They know that people, despite being holed up all winter, or dehydrated to practically nothing after the drought of summer, do have cash squirreled away. These business people are aware, being fellow addicts, that a serious quilter is always in withdrawal, always desperate for more fabric to finish a quilt or stuff up the stash. The fully stocked shop, with its knowledgeable employees, is central to this ongoing addiction. Workers help steer customers to the latest bolts of cloth to hit the store, match fabrics or whatever is needed to make the next quilt project a real eye-popper.

Those who work in a quilt store – sometimes referred to as a guilt store – also serve as interpreters for novices and the occasional male who ventures inside. Terms like "fat quarters," "fancy cut" and "strip quilting" usually mean something different to men than to women quilters. And if quilters aren't moving out and about, the new goodies don't move out the door. For the owner of a fabric store, staging a quilt hop/rendezvous/safari means money in.

Why would the Montana Highway Patrol give a hoot about some quilt hop/rendezvous/safari? Because they know anytime there are people traveling up and down the highway like hot winds out of You Know Where, it means money for the state coffers. Big time. Especially for those of us driving vehicles with out-of-state license plates.

I know how our car hums down the road when I'm going the speed limit in Montana. Oregon speed limit is 70 mph. Eastern Montana's is 75 to 80 mph. Whee hee! I also know how easy it is for my foot to press down on the gas pedal just a teeny bit because the next quilt store is a good ways off. You cannot tell me a bunch of women, squeezed into a car and zooming by us on I-90/I-94, are on their frenzied way to a sheep auction. Nope. These females are bent on getting to the next quilt store and before me if possible.

"We'll see you at the next stop" really means "eat my dust" to fellow hoppers.

What's a state trooper to do? Plenty.

Under no circumstances, though, should said trooper slip into a quilt store and ask questions. That would get the wind up, and within 30 minutes every participating store would know the MHP has sniffed something out. Once the cover is blown this news will travel to each participating store's regular customers faster than a runaway calf.

With an eye toward protecting the public, and also an eye toward some easy income for the state, the MHP could send a spouse, significant other or the pastor's spouse into the nearest quilt shop the month before it usually starts. The trooper's snooper could ferret out when the quilt hop is scheduled to run and obtain a map of the route. But be forewarned as well, MHP. If you have loved ones who quilt, the babes you bust might be your own.

A quilt hop is a lot of fun for all the participants. Think of it as a good-natured looting. We quilters make off with some incredible new fabrics and other goodies, quilt store owners rake in bundles of cash, and the state of Montana increases its revenue. As for me, I'm already making plans for the next heist…I mean hop. I intend to drive within the law, but if I slip up, fine me within an inch of my fanny, MHP, but don't take away my quilt hop passport or my Visa, please. That's all I ask.

Say What?

People from many regions in the United States have their way of saying things, and that includes the folks from eastern Montana.

"I'm lugging rocks out of the barrow pit," my Fallon neighbor told me one day. I assumed she was talking about an area of the farm where wheelbarrows are stored. It seemed odd wheelbarrows would be stored in a pit. Sounded like a lot of work to me, hoisting a wheelbarrow out of a hole in the ground every time you needed to use it. Also, I couldn't figure out why rocks should be in such a place. On the other hand, I knew eastern Montana soil grew rocks better than anything else, except weeds and rattlesnakes, so it made sense rocks might sprout up in the wheelbarrow storage area and have to be removed every now and then.

"I'm mowing my barrow pit," commented another neighbor. It was close to spring branding time. Say what? First they store wheelbarrows in a crater, one that grows rocks, and now they have to mow it, too? I know folks here take pride in their places. They want everything tidied up for when neighbors and relatives come for social things such as weddings, brandings, decorating graves and the like. But isn't this a little much? I didn't ask how someone mows a barrow pit. I left it alone.

The terms "dinner" and "supper" are good examples of how two plain words mean different things depending on where a body comes from. Dinner and supper mean the same thing in my part of Oregon. Whether it's a big meal, like roast turkey with all the trimmings, or a light snack, it's the final meal of the day. The first time I invited the Montana relatives to dinner and gave them the time, it caused a fluster almost as big as a mama cow missing her calf.

"Now, when you invited us to dinner, did you mean dinner? Or supper?" Shirley asked. As *the* female first cousin, she was feeling it out for the rest of them.

"Dinner," I replied, "or supper."

By this point in the conversation this lifelong farm-woman realized she was dealing with an ignorant relative from the big city, one who did not know the value of feeding time.

"When we say dinner, we mean the noon meal, at 12 o'clock sharp," she told me.

"Oh!" I replied. "We call it lunch back home." I wracked my brain and wondered. Had we arrived, lugging a hot dish of BBQ beans, or platter of fresh-baked dinner rolls for suppertime, only to find the meal occurred earlier and at high noon?

There are certain idioms specific to eastern Montanans. The term idiom is not the plural form of idiot. An idiom is a language or phrase typical of a region or peoples. A newcomer, one with at least a few functioning brain cells, learns the local idioms so he or she doesn't act like an idiot, and that is the only way these two words relate to each other.

I have learned the importance of a nut bucket at a branding, and that these nuts do not go into my favorite recipe of chocolate chip cookies. As it is, I doubt the little bulls would want them to go anywhere.

When a rancher tells the hired hand to go out and haul some cake, it is not a dessert item. This sort of cake consists of ground-up food cattle would normally eat, such as alfalfa hay, corn, or wheat. The goop is heated and then compressed into pellets about the size of large walnut. Make no mistake, those critters do like their cake.

"When you drop cake on the ground, you better get out of the way fast," my husband said. "A person risks getting trampled by the cows, they love it so much."

A sundog is not the latest brand of fancy, earth-friendly sandal hot out of southern California, but a brilliant rainbow-like happening in the sky.

A relative told my husband at coffee one morning he was going to go plow some guess rows. Guess rows?

Was he guessing he's planting corn but hopes it doesn't come up sugar beets? Does it take him four or five rows of planting before he realizes he's in the right field or not? Maybe working up the guess rows helps him forget he is supposed to be fixing the washing machine, not piddling around in the field.

This latest idiom puzzled me all the way to Billings and back. Guess rows, I've found, are the spacings between the rows in the middle of the field, made when the tractor turns to go back where it came from, and start the next row loop. It took me two tries and one sketch on paper before I got straight the meaning of this one.

I've noticed there's interesting information passed around at the daily morning coffee.

"Your cousin's husband plans to go out and bleed some cattle today," Wayne told me at breakfast some time back.

My mouth stayed closed. There's a Proverb in the Bible that says if a fool keeps his mouth shut, others will think him wise, and that's a no-fooling smart saying. But I felt for the cows. How long would they let the poor critters bleed?

"They're taking blood samples from the cattle to test for diseases," he said, as if reading my gory thoughts. Phew! At least I won't have to get down on my knees and pray for those poor creatures.

What Montana folks call moisture, looks to me like good Oregon rain. When it does moisture, the locals rejoice because everything is usually dry as a bone. But then they worry because too much moisture will turn the roads to a sticky goo they call gumbo. I'm a recycled home economist, but I do know true gumbo is made with okra. I've yet to see okra growing in anyone's garden in Montana, let alone in the roads.

Then there is rattle corn. Rattle corn is the name given for too mature, too dry table corn, but cooked up and served anyway. The relatives call it such because it rattles around in the mouth while trying to be chewed. I will leave that one right where it sits. I have enough confusion about all those local idioms rattling around in my head as it is.

I finally solved the mystery of the barrow pit. I asked someone.

"When there's rain or snow, the excess moisture runs off the roadway and into it," she told me.

"Oh, you mean a drainage ditch," I replied. She nodded, as if explaining to a small child. So that's what they've been talking about all this time. If they would just say what I mean, it would be so much easier.

Breaking Her In

There are two sides to every story. Remember this the next time you hear someone brag about his or her first ride on a horse.

Some things in life must be endured. Someone trying to learn to ride a horse is one of them.

I saw her coming, prancing along on stubby, thick legs. By the looks of her belly fat, I'd say she hadn't had many workouts, or been taken for a run in a long time. Her hair looked thin, and it stood up on end between her short ears. She showed a pretty color at least. Wearing a small nose and a big mouth, she let it be known to the cowboys, the poor dogs and any stray horse standing around that she had no intention of going for a little horseback ride today.

We had all moseyed through a pleasant day branding cows, visiting and filling our bellies with good food. Not content with the day's work done, or the peaceful

atmosphere, some idiot with a cow-poop-filled head pro-
posed both she and I go for a little ride. Maybe I should
feel sorry for her. I bet this critter had been roped into
the "let's learn to get on a horse and go for a little ride"
conversation many times before. I could have told her I
was in no mood for this sort of foolishness either.

At the mention of the idea, she put up a fuss. Her
neck stiffened, she jerked that nose back and forth and
then started making loud noises at every person and animal in sight. It looked to me like this was one nag who
didn't want to get on with the business of what it takes
to ride a horse. Worse, she looked old enough to be put
out to pasture, and that's no lie. While a cowboy settled
her down, I stood there, quiet, so she wouldn't scare even
more. Even with that one cowboy helping for all he was
worth, it took forever to get us connected and in the saddle. She kept that hind end of hers, which looked like two
big watermelons glued together, moving around in the
saddle. For a while we couldn't meet in the middle, but it
finally happened.

There we stood, she on my poor, aching back and me
expected to give her a nice little ride.

Despite my load, I got us moving, slow and gentle,
around on the grassy piece outside the corral. I wanted to
present a dignified presence, and no way was I going to

let her pull some greenhorn stunt and make me look like a fool's first cousin.

After a little bit, I knew she'd called it a day because noises started coming out of her tooth-filled mouth again, and her massive rear end began twitching back and forth in the saddle. She wanted off, she announced. It was fine with me. I tried to keep from grinning ear to ear when my favorite cow gal came and rescued me.

"You're a good boy," she whispered in my ear, as she patted my neck and snuck a treat in my mouth. My gal said other things to me, but I have my dignity, and a smart horse knows when to keep his mouth shut, so we'll let what passed between us be something on the order of, "It's not every day you have to give an overweight old lady her first ride, but you did a good job."

I saw that greenhorn gal swing her big rear end away, telling others what a good job she'd done. That female didn't do anything! She had to be helped into the saddle, and that was a sight to behold in itself. It took two grown men, including her poor husband, two tries before they pushed her up and then shoved her into the saddle. After that hallelujah effort, she sat there, making squawking noises with that mouth of hers while I did the real work. She didn't even thank me for the nice, easy ride, let alone give me a treat. Now my back hurts like the dickens, which is the nice version of what my cowboy buddies would say.

I don't feel sorry for her. I promise you, if she manages to get that big rump of hers on my back again, there's one woman who better hang on tight.

Like I said, some things in life a body just has to endure, and one of them is being roped into giving an oversized, big-jawed woman a horseback ride.

Coffee Time

Coffee time is a daily ritual for a lot of men and women in rural parts of Montana. Whether alone, or with others, it is part of the rhythm of their lives. Social or not, the fact remains for many, if there is no morning cuppa, there is no get-up-and-go-a for the rest of the day.

Area people have attended morning coffee in downtown Fallon for decades. These days, my husband goes the first shift as often as he can during the weeks we are in residence. Coffee time gives him the opportunity to visit with some of the people who live and farm in the community. When he returns, my first words to him are the same each time.

"How did it go at coffee?"

The early birds gather at 6 a.m. in a small room on the main street. In recent years, the volunteer fire department purchased the old building and spruced it up. The routine is the same each day. First one there makes the coffee. People pay into a money can, 50 cents a day, for the right to drink. This cash keeps the hot fresh-brewed coffee coming, the lights on and everyone buzzed. Locals keep the place tidy, and they treat it with respect.

For these people, there is no such thing as a mocha, skinny latte or flavored coffee, and it wouldn't be smart asking the fellas as to whether the coffee was made with organic fair-trade beans. The only beans these guys care about are the ones growing in their fields. Any mention of fair trade and crops in the same breath just might bring on a hollering match, or a fistfight.

The coffee, and it better be Folgers caffeinated, is brewed strong, looks as black as a grease can and is served straight up. Take it or leave it.

This pleasant habit of meeting people and drinking coffee puzzled me when we first moved to Fallon. My parents were not coffee drinkers. They rarely gathered with others just to sit, guzzle coffee and yak. I drank the coffee in our faculty room during my teaching years, but it was a grab and go. With two-dozen or so squirrely fourth-graders, a body had better stay alert, or suffer the consequences. But really, why meet every single day of the week, including Sunday, and at the crack of dawn?

"The tradition of meeting people for coffee is to find out what's going on," cousin Shirley told me over coffee. "If I stay away, I might miss something." Shirley is the only female attending Fallon's early-bird brew time, which says a lot about her persevering nature.

That something missed might add up to a lot. At coffee, people pass on community news, debate issues of the day, find out the latest information about ranching or crops, exchange gossip or rustle up some help with a chore. This ritual offers individuals within the community the opportunity to stay connected with each other, especially during the frozen months of winter. The regulars wouldn't miss it for the world, and if one of them does, everyone wonders. Ears perk up, and one or two might even drive by the member's place to see if everything is OK.

Coffee time is also a chance for people to tell stories about themselves or others, and it serves as a perfect location to pull a practical joke or two.

One morning as Wayne debriefed me on the daily news learned at the community caffeine klatch, he told me about a prank some of the guys pulled on my cousin, Don, a few years earlier.

Don owns a hardtop '75 Nova SS, two-door. "The kind of car men my age would kill for," Wayne said.

Don kept the Nova in an insulated outbuilding because he is a man who protects his automotive treasures. The citizens of Fallon planned an upcoming auction, with proceeds donated to a charitable cause. Some of the 6 a.m. regulars found one of the auction flyers. They decided to alter it to include Don's 1975 Nova. This prank points out one of the dangers of drinking hard, hot coffee so early in the morning: Slumbering brains wake up.

At the next coffee, the guys just happened to have the flyer available for everyone to check out. Don looked over the list. When he spied his beloved car as one of the items to be auctioned, he got really worked up. The boys eventually told him it was only a joke. It wouldn't have surprised anyone if he went home, checked the Nova to make sure it was safe and then, to get his heart rate under control, slugged down something more potent than a shot of black coffee.

My husband developed serious heart problems late spring 2013. He couldn't go to Montana in May, so I flew to Billings and then drove east. While there, one of the regulars let me know he was drinking Wayne's share of morning coffee as well as his, and to inform Wayne his coffee bill was at $40 and rising. I told that honest businessman if he wanted Wayne to pay the debt, on our next trip out my hubby would squat outside the gent's store in downtown Terry and hold up a cardboard sign advertising his coffee debt. To do things right, Wayne would also have a big empty coffee can ready for donations from people ambling around downtown. There's nothing like panhandling the good folks of Terry to stir up business, or stir up something else.

Coffee anyone?

Dogs Working Me

The bitterroot is Montana's official state flower. The agate and the sapphire are the official state rocks. From my way of looking at it, the official state dog is the border collie.

I was mostly unfamiliar with this breed until we moved to Montana part-time. People raise sheep near us in Crabtree, Oregon, and I saw border collies working as sheep dogs, but only at a distance. A border collie is a smart dog. If you find yourself in the company of this type of pooch, it is wise to remember some things. A border collie is observant. Nothing escapes from under the nose of the dog. When in the presence of a border collie I have learned to pay attention, because that dog pays attention to me.

Border collies are working dogs, first and foremost. They are born and bred to herd. The animal decides the area of his/her territory, and then works like crazy to control whoever or whatever is inside this space. Collies think of strategies to maneuver, and if necessary, outwit the critters in their care. This breed makes good guard dogs for small children and other helpless and/or clueless humans.

Another of the border collie's tasks is to guard the perimeter of his or her territory. An on-duty border collie is all business. Step near his or her territory's edge and you can expect growls, barking or worse. As I see it, the teeth of a border collie look exactly like the teeth of a wolf. Nowadays, if I spot a border collie on patrol duty, I give that dog a lot of space. The dog minds his business; I mind mine. A person might get chummy with a border collie, but only after the owner of the dog shows his animal the new human being is part of the group. Then, and only then, is the newbie allowed inside the collie's territory. Maybe. Do not be foolish enough to think once a body is allowed on a border collie's turf, the individual can go about her merry business. Inside the dog's working space, the collie will use every bit of intelligence, every wily strategy and boundless energy to get the new critter to do what he or she wants done. With some, the dog must work hard to accomplish this; with other folks, the dog knows it is going to be an easy bit of work.

Shirley and her husband, Dan, acquired a male border collie named Cowboy some years back. When I learned Cowboy's mother herded chickens out in the country, it became clear why this dog shined up to me right away. From the beginning, Cowboy probably took one look at me and thought, *two legs, with hair like feathers sticking out all over its head. Cackles a lot too. This chick's gonna be easy to work.*

The first time I came to visit my cousin after Cowboy became the alpha dog on the place, he immediately sensed I did not come to play with him. But that strong-willed dog had plans for me.

Before I had taken four steps from the car, the hyper piece of fur dashed around the side of the house. He re-appeared with a small ball held between a set of large, handsome teeth. I swiftly calculated a dog with his teeth wrapped around a ball would be less likely to bite me, and I relaxed a bit. Cowboy sensed my self-disarmament and made his next move. He positioned himself in front of the porch steps. If I moved one way, he moved in front of me. After a few dogged but failed maneuvers on my part, I realized this oversized pup wanted to play. No way I would put a hand into that gaping, slobbery mouth loaded with sharp teeth and retrieve the ball.

After some furious pointing to the ground on my part, Cowboy dropped his toy at my feet. He pointed to the ball with his long nose, while swiveling his eyeballs upward. Those large innocent-looking eyes gazed into mine. You could almost see the wheels whizzing inside his canine cranium. Could Cowboy read my mind? His body language needed no translation.

Sister, you twitch so much as a nostril, and I will coun-teract your move. Keeping that in mind, shall we play a little ball?

I kicked the ball into the air. Cowboy chased it like a streak of Montana lightning, snagging it his mouth like a major league player. I served another kick, and then another. Sometimes, and to show off a bit, he jumped high in the air, then swooped down like a hawk on a wild rabbit, nailing it every time. It dawned on me, after quite a spell of the kick-and-catch game, this gal would be play-ing some tedious rounds of Slobber Ball before there was any chance of getting inside the house. I had a problem on my hands. The shrewd dog planned to work me good. A tenacious and energetic dog, Cowboy intended to play ball until feeding time, or I dropped dead. I did make it into the house on that visit, but only after Shirley came outside and give Cowboy a good scolding for monopoliz-ing my time, energy and wits.

Not only does a border collie work like a dog to con-trol a perimeter and to rule all creatures both great and small inside its borders, this breed has sensitive feelings. A border collie builds a close relationship with his or her owner, and if someone tries to insert herself between those two, the dog's nose gets out of joint.

When cousin Dave, a seasoned bachelor, delivered a large rock to decorate my yard in Fallon, he brought his dog, Oreo, with him. Sporting thick stripes of black and white fur, the dog did vaguely resemble a big, hairy Oreo cookie.

As I oohed and aahed over the rock, I noticed Oreo would not look at me. If I said his name or reached out my hand, he kept his magnificent head turned away. No matter how I tried, he would not acknowledge my presence. Unbeknownst to me, I had broken at least three serious pup protocols. I had not greeted Oreo first or given him affection in a proper manner. I then proceeded to exclude him from the conversation between us human beings. Adding another insult to the growing pile, I had hugged Oreo's owner. Right under the pup's nose, too. When I realized my faux pas, it was too late to make amends. I had ruffled the fur of *the* dog. I tried to correct the situation by speaking words to the pooch, words that conveyed the promise None of This Will Happen Again! Sadly, I knew it might take me the rest of my life, or his, to win Oreo's trust. Maybe. Dogs remember.

Still a novice about the complex nature of a border collie, and in the spirit of self-preservation with Cowboy, I developed a trick or two of my own. When it was visiting time with Shirley, I put into operation my dog-fooling strategy.

First, I parked my rig as close to the front porch as allowable, but not too close to arouse Cowboy's suspicions.

Once I exited the vehicle and with purse clutched tight, Cowboy appeared, as prompt as the town gossip and with the disgusting-looking ball between his jaws. We both knew the routine. I pointed to the ground. He dropped the ball. I kicked the ball. He snagged the ball. We played the game for a few rounds, enough for me to dupe him into thinking he was working me, fool him into thinking he was in control of the game. Without warning and during a lot of two-faced double-talk, I kicked his toy as hard as I could in the direction opposite the front door. While Cowboy galloped after the ball, I ran like fury up the porch steps, swung open the door and practically leaped inside the house. Although winded, as it was hefty exercise running up a set of stairs like that for this aging lady, I congratulated myself. My dog-fooling worked.

But when it was time for me to leave and go home, there sat Cowboy in front of my car door, slime-covered ball in his big, toothy mouth. His soft-looking but deceitful eyes stared into mine. I stared back. While we eyeballed each other, I truly believe that smart pup grinned at me and when he did, I knew what he was thinking, "Play ball?"

A Silver Spoon

Years ago, a silver spoon turned out to be the golden opportunity one auctioneer needed to move the goods at a country sale. This event occurred at the site of our home in Fallon, but decades before we bought the place. The lady of the house planned to move away, and she needed to get rid of unwanted possessions. The auctioneer hired to do the job noticed something odd. This woman owned an uncommon number of corsets.

I think a sadistic man invented the contraption.

A corset is a long, tight-fitting undergarment, reinforced by pieces of bone or some other rigid material. In centuries past, both men and women wore corsets, often decorative, but the female of the species used them more often, and did so until recent decades.

A corset had lacings and when cinched up encased a woman from her hips to her boobs. The entrapped lady, while enduring the agony, hoped to appear more slim and trim to others, especially gentlemen callers. Think of the movie, "Gone with the Wind". There stands poor Scarlett, while Mammy vigorously pulls tighter and tighter the strings of her corset. Wearing one must have been pure torture, especially during the hot months of the year, and all for vanity.

The corsets at this auction might have been new, or maybe used. That bit of fact is lost to history. They were out of fashion by this time, however, and that proved a dilemma to the auctioneer.

How to unload all those corsets?

Ken Hess from Miles City held the sale and told me the tale. If Ken tells a story, I have learned, it must be the complete and unadulterated truth. Hess' task required he auction off both the house and its contents.

"She had a boatload of corsets," Hess recalled.

Before the auction, one of the potential buyers, a woman, found a silver spoon somewhere within the other items. Hess watched as she picked it up and then hid it inside one of the boxes of corsets. After awhile, another gal, rummaging through the boxes of corsets, found the spoon and tucked it into another box of the stomach squeezers. Hess watched this happen a number of times, but he kept quiet. Later, when no one noticed, he went through the boxes, found the spoon and slipped it into his pocket.

When it came time to auction the corsets, bidding became brisk. He auctioned off every one of those boxes of corsets for 10 to 12 dollars apiece. After they were all sold to the smug women, Hess pulled the silver spoon out of his pocket.

"Now," he told the crowd, "we sell the spoon."

The coveted and illusive item went for 12 dollars.

"Boy, I sold a lot of corsets that day," Hess recalled, "and for 12 bucks a box."

It makes a person wonder. What did all those modern gals *do* with their boxes of old-time corsets?

All Aboard!

Often, when a person thinks of a railroad engineer, a stereotypical image comes to mind. He is a burly man who wears a striped cap, red kerchief around his neck and big leather gloves. The gentleman rides in the engine with one hand resting on the open window. When pedestrians wave to him, he waves back as the train roars on by.

I never met a genuine railroad engineer until we came to Montana. When it happened, I did not see, standing in front of me, a man wearing a hat and kerchief. In his place stood Carla Allen.

Allen is a petite woman, quiet and gentle natured. She did not quite fit my mental image of someone who could ride herd over a 225,000-pound engine as it pounded down the track, but that is exactly what she does for a living.

When she climbs aboard the 1814, or any of the other five engines owned by Central Montana Rail, Allen is the lady in charge. This native Montanan is not only chief locomotive engineer, but she is the general manager for the CMR, headquartered in Denton.

Allen was not always interested in the railroad business or in trains.

"I never paid attention to them when I was a kid," Allen said. "I didn't ride a train until I went to work for the Central Montana Rail." But the railroad played a major part during her early life.

Allen grew up in the tiny railroad town of Denton. Her paternal grandmother, Bertha Swenson, homesteaded land at Bear Spring Bench north of Denton. She later married another homesteader, Carl Erlandson. Allen's father, Erlan "Babe" Erlandson, worked for 30 years as track foreman for the Milwaukee and for the Burlington Northern railroads.

After college and marriage, Allen moved back to her hometown. In the mid-1980s, this stay-at-home mom found the railroad knocking at her door. Her kids were in school, so she agreed to work in the office. Before long, Allen ended up on the track as well.

"We're a small company, so everyone pitches in, whether it's a repair of the track or running the train," Allen said. After a year of apprenticeship, Allen found herself behind the controls of a massive engine, making her one of the first women engineers in that part of Montana.

After I met Allen, I learned about trains and how important they are to isolated farmers and ranchers. The CMR is a short line. A short line railroad operates like a shuttle, and its role is critical for transporting grain crops to market, especially from remote areas in central Montana.

CMR engines pull cars loaded with grain or other agricultural products from either Denton or Geraldine to Moccasin. From Moccasin the Burlington Northern Santa Fe moves the load to somewhere in the Pacific Northwest, often for export.

"Some of our wheat also goes to flour mills," Allen said. A person living in other parts of the United States is likely to find central Montana wheat, a type of hard wheat high in protein and gluten, in the local deli's loaf of bread or lunchtime bagel.

Besides hauling crops to market, the engines are used for the varied Charlie Russell Chew Choo dinner train experiences during the spring, summer and fall months of the year. On these themed train trips, people are the load, but the destination is a remote area of central Montana. The train guests eat, visit, view gorgeous scenery, get entertained, and then are hauled back to Denton. At Christmas, one engine, be it the 1814 or one of the others, is selected to run The North Pole Adventure excursions.

"We are always sold out for these Christmas excursions," Allen told me. "They are more popular than ever. We had 12 excursions in 2016 and plan for 13 in 2017."

The CMR, in existence for 30 years, is the result of a broken promise and shows how determined Montanans responded to the problem.

Burlington Northern Railroad bought the Lewistown-Denton-Geraldine spur from the Milwaukee Railroad in 1980. After the purchase, Burlington Northern promised to continue serving farmers and ranchers in that area of central Montana. But later the railroad thought it too expensive to keep up that part of the track and planned to vacate it. In plain words, Burlington Northern planned to abandon both the track and the promise. That's when some folks from Montana made up their minds it was time to stand up to the railroad.

The result? The CMR came into being in 1986. The state of Montana became owners of that part of the track, and Burlington Northern coughed up money, equipment and training for the personnel necessary to run the new, cooperatively-owned railway. Local people like Allen stepped in to make the new company a success.

What's it like to drive the massive blue and white engine down the track?

"It's quite a sensation, feeling the engine working hard, pulling loaded cars filled with grain," Allen said.

The CMR works "on demand." When local farmers and ranchers need grain shipped out, the railroad loads the harvest. Allen picks up and delivers around 5,200 tons of grain during a normal day of transport during the season, which runs from October until April. Track repair and maintenance take place during the summer months.

Allen's day on the track starts busy.

"The first thing we do is fill out a track warrant permit," she said. "The permit allows us to use the main track, and only for that day."

A thorough check of the engine is next. Allen wants a safe trip. She inspects brakes, generator, running gear, headlight and knuckles.

Trains and knuckles didn't make sense to me at first, but Allen explained the knuckle is the part that couples the cars together. A faulty knuckle means the cars could separate. Allen and her crew change head and ditch lights, wash windows and do other needed maintenance. She not only wants the engine safe; Allen never wants it thirsty.

"These engines were built around 1952," she said. "Old engines like this use a lot of diesel oil. We never change the oil, like in an automobile. We only add oil."

Once the engine and cars pass inspection, it's "all aboard."

The railway track runs according to the geography of the land. This means Allen and her crew never know what's on the track ahead.

"One time, as we traveled through Sage Creek tunnel, we saw a family of raccoons on the track," she said, "so we stopped the train until they were safely off to the side." Deer, rattlesnakes and other critters find their way onto the track as well. Then there's the occasional boulder, or drifts of snow during the colder months. If it rains a lot, there is the danger of mudslides or the track separating from its bed.

As chief engineer, it's Allen's responsibility to put her engine to bed at the end of a working day.

"We check it all over, making sure it has enough oil and water," she said. "Then I run the engine into the shop and shut it down."

Is this grey-haired grandma ready to retire?

"Not yet," Allen replied with a smile. "I love to be outdoors and see the scenery. Besides, my husband thinks I love the smell of diesel oil too much to retire just yet."

Wicked Women and
Ornery Outlaws

Many people enjoy watching a good stage play. To be drawn into a story recreated by skilled actors is a treat to see, hear and experience.

I had never experienced a dinner theater production until my husband and I attended an event during our early years in Montana. It didn't happen in a restaurant or a theater. The play took place, in part, on a vintage railroad train called the Charlie Russell Chew-Choo Dinner Train. Although our ride happened years ago, the chefs, waiters and actors still do their stuff for willing but unwitting passengers on this unique train excursion. Come along with me for an interesting ride and a peek at some old-time wicked women and their ornery outlaw buddies.

The ride on the Charlie Russell Chew-Choo started out tame enough. We gathered at the loading spot, Kingston Junction, about nine miles north of Lewistown, Montana. Our small group consisted of my husband, two of my first cousins and their spouses.

The train departed at 4 p.m. The on-board commentator announced we would travel on a 28-mile round trip ride to Denton and back. Promises of rare views of part of the massive central Montana landscape, a prime rib dinner and "special entertainment" fueled our interest. The chance to see the country on a beautiful autumn afternoon and squeeze in a bit of family visiting while dining on good food – what more could there be?

Lots more.

To view the train up close is an experience. Each 1950s vintage railcar is made of stainless steel and weighs 60 tons. Originally from Massachusetts and with an automatic transmission, now each engine car is powered by diesel fuel and pulls the Chew-Choo cars at 25 mph. Despite its slower pace during these special rides, it doesn't take a lot of imagination to see why the massive size and speed of a locomotive dazzled people in earlier times. For some of us, they still do. To add to the sense of intrigue, once the engine moved down the track, everyone on board knew he or she was part of a captive audience. Indeed, the Charlie Russell Chew-Choo served as the perfect setting for a western-style dinner theater experience.

While we chugged out of Kingston, local musicians greeted the guests, built the atmosphere and kept us entertained. Waiters served up coffee, other drinks and our dinner salads. Warm, fragrant yeast rolls proved good company to a thick, medium-rare prime rib. While we ate, the commentator directed our attention to scenic highlights and history specific to this piece of central Montana. For me, a woman raised in Portland, Oregon, this first view of the vast panorama of blue sky, massive mountains and prairie typical to that part of the state proved to be awe-inspiring.

Our train traveled on a piece of the old Milwaukee Railroad. Years ago, this line ran from Lewistown to Great Falls. Built in 1913 and now owned by Central Montana Rail, the 137-mile track is still in use. Carla Allen, manager of the CMR, served as engineer for this ride.

We were barely into our beef when the announcer, in somber tones, told us we were passing by the Bull's Eye Saloon, reputed to be the hangout of the nasty and notorious Salt Creek Gang. The women were wicked, it was whispered, and the outlaws ornery as old rattlesnakes. All of them, he cautioned, were nothing more than a bunch of thieves. I looked out the window and took in the bare and isolated landscape surrounding the supposed saloon. The raw wood siding on the small den of iniquity looked fairly new, and to me it could have passed for a Montana branch of the IRS. To be safe, I made sure my purse was out of sight as our train moved past the building.

On the way to Denton, we traveled over three spectacular trestles, saw the old railroad town sites of Ware and Hoosac (a few hardy folks still lived there) and then the train burrowed through Sage Creek Tunnel. As I looked at these nearly deserted towns and isolated homesteader shacks, I could not help but wonder about the history of this desolate part of the West. What was it like, back then, living in this lonesome area? How did people survive the merciless beating of the sun's rays during the long, sweltering days of a Montana summer, or horribly frigid winter storms as they roared down from the Rockies?

At Denton, the engine car switched ends, and we began chugging back to Kingston Junction. The gentle rocking of the train, like a slow-moving ship at sea, promised all passengers a relaxing end to the journey. There was no sign of those outlaws. What happened to the theater part of this dinner? As my curiosity floated out the window, the train slowed down. Quick as a hawk landing on a chick, a red-hot-looking woman, named Cherry, flanked by her snuff-chewing buddies, climbed aboard. We were, as the over-worn phrase states, surrounded by outlaws. Where did all those scruffy-looking people come from? While slinging sly looks to her men, Cherry smeared another layer of bright-red lipstick on already overdressed lips. She dropped the tube down her ample and open front.

"When I saw her reload, I knew something was about to happen," Wayne later told me. At the time of the take-over, my husband scrunched himself up, and then pressed himself, flat as a sandwich board, against the window of the railroad car.

"Is there a fella here named Dan Dukart?" asked the woman in red. The rest of the men in our railroad car laughed, nervous-like. I heard catcalls. Men with rifles stood at each end of the car's opening.

"He's over there," someone hollered. "Over there" meant the man sitting across from me. Cherry —that poor woman would come down with a chest cold dressed like that —knew right where her star victim sat. The honky-tonk female looked straight at her victim. How'd she know that? What was next?

Smack! Cherry landed a least one good smooch on Dan's cheek, then another. She left her bright-red brand on him, and with no shame whatsoever. Poor Dan, trapped between his wife, Shirley, and Cherry, had no way to turn, except red. I just kept taking photos while folks laughed and hooted, and the other captive men read the handwriting on the wall. For all I knew, my husband had sunk down under the seat, but she'd have to climb over me to get him. Being of ample build myself, Wayne was safe, wherever he was. After she worked Dan over, Cherry left him to hunt for new prey. Other bandits, the ones wearing more clothes, worked the passengers as well. After an indecent interval, the gang went outdoors. Something was up, and it was not Cherry's bodice, that was for sure.

We witnessed a hearty, real-looking shootout — wild horseback riding, smoking pistols, bushwhacking rifles and all. I had to give the gang credit. That bunch of crooks knew how to properly do each other in. There was no honesty among this group of thieves. From where I sat it looked like Cherry was faring better than her bosom buddies with the beards, who dropped on the ground around her like piles of dead flies. I'm not sure where she'd hid her firearms beforehand, but from the looks of things Cherry must have played things pretty close to her chest.

This part of the play lasted a good while, and from the safety of being inside the train, it was enjoyable to watch the dudes hit the dirt. While bodies littered the outside of the Bull's Eye Saloon, and Cherry checked to make sure she still had all her assets, the train started up again. Kingston Junction soon came into sight. It was the end of a great, almost-four-hour train ride.

Later, I discovered local farmers and ranchers served as the actors. They took time and energy to organize this little bit of live-action theater, despite a heavy workload in real life. Besides having a good time, their efforts revealed a sincere dedication to amateur acting.

But there is one thing that puzzled me. If Cherry and her group of thespians were volunteers, folks who had never seen us before, why did I spot real $10 bills peeking out of that wicked woman's bodacious bosom just before she lip-smacked Dan? I think one of those rascals from Fallon slipped her the money because it sure looked like a setup to me.

Outside Inventory

I often wonder why some people hang on to everything they ever possessed.

My dad practiced this odd behavior his entire adult life. If someone looked to the east side of our yard in Portland, a rusting '33 Oldsmobile and a '47 Ford blocked the view. Swing the head in a northerly direction, and there sat both the '50 and '53 Fords. Let's not count the boat, wood trailer, and an empty doghouse large enough to hold an entire Iditarod team. Moving south on the property, there sat decaying rabbit hutches and the remnants of a huge WWII tent, blackened with mold, rotting and draped, like the specter of death, over a significant part of our backyard. His old, decades-empty herd of hog pens squatted under a huge fir tree a stone's throw from our western neighbors. Near the pens stood a dilapidated chicken coop topped with a rotting roof. Our two acres in the city served as a museum/holding site/cemetery for my father's many vehicles, past interests and collections.

Back to vehicles in particular, he also parked the corroded remnants of his old Essex on a large vacant lot we owned on the next block. A smart move, because by that point in time dad had over-vexed the patience of my mother. Right up to my wedding day, his collections of debris proved a source embarrassment to me. Why do such a thing? In particular, holding on to anything with tires, but now useless?

During one of our monthlong stays in Fallon, I connected the dots.

Both of my mother's brothers stored, in the yard by the house, the barn or in outlying pastures, their farm vehicles, hay equipment, mowers and any other implement pulled or pushed by horses, tractors or human beings. As each one farmed for more than half a century, thought processes must work from that fact outward to adequately grasp the scope of their collections.

"Farmers tend to leave it in a field, where it died, but out of the path of normal farm operations," my husband noted. By this time, having cleared out all his deceased father-in-law's mountains of junk, the man knew what he was talking about.

My father, I finally realized, behaved like a frustrated city farmer. I'm not blaming my uncles for my father's behavior, not at all. Dad was well versed in the practice of obtaining outside inventory years before he set his size 13 boots on Montana sod. Dad hoarded stuff. My uncles' ways of managing equipment gave him some new ideas is all, tidbits he could take back to Oregon and then put into practice. But if you think about it from the farmer or rancher's point of view, this way of doing things makes sense.

A farm or ranch is often miles from town. If something breaks down, whether a truck, corn wagon or tractor, the farmer can't afford to burn either daylight or gas fetching a new part. Instead, the guy or gal ambles over to one of the broken-down rigs napping nearby, removes the necessary part, fixes the problem and gets back to work. It's simple. Move parts from one vehicle to the other. An observer must admit there is logic to this way of keeping spare parts on hand. The person better remember, however, which Peter has been robbed to pay which Paul. If the farmer's collection of out-of-commission machinery lacks what is needed, chances are good another farmer nearby has it. However, there is one rule for taking from the other person's outside inventory. Well-mannered, honest folks ask permission before they trespass to lift stuff from someone's tractor, truck, implement or scrap lumber. The others? They just grab it and run.

Hanging onto every piece of iron also saves time and energy. If the yard around the house and barn is chock full of stuff, this means there is less lawn to fertilize, water and mow. No use wasting effort caring for a stretch of useless grass. Leaving items to lie where they died also teaches farm kids to be resourceful, careful and creative. Only a roaming boy knows what great things can be built with some forgotten tools lurking inside the cab of a dead and decaying farm truck. Many a young farm gal, like my Mom, learned to stay on her feet while walking atop an outbuilding, all the while keeping a watchful eye on the rusted debris parked and packed on the ground below. With a kid's imagination, the old '42 Chevy pickup becomes a space ship, ready to blast off to Mars, the moon or Miles City.

Our biannual drive from Oregon to eastern Montana has its tedious moments, but when I spot a decrepit, deserted farmhouse at the edge of the horizon, my spirits perk up. I know near the old abandoned home, its weathered wood bleached a dove gray, often sits a rusted pickup or tractor. If I am lucky, the yard and pasture will be littered with stuff, all leftovers from human lives now spent. For a moment I imagine life on that farm during its days of productivity, with kids running around in the yard, a woman hanging clothes on a clothesline, and the farmer with his head buried deep under the hood of a John Deere, Fordson or Cockshutt.

As our car zooms past the deserted homestead, I take a good look and smile to myself. Whether it is pride in

owning something with an engine, or simple practical-
ity, some people, like my father, cannot let go of their
equipment. Or maybe it is the other way around. The old
tractor or baler, even after all these years, cannot let go of
the place it made a difference in this world, the place it
reigned as king: the family farm.

Yard Art

On our journeys to and from Montana, I notice more and more breathtaking yard art made from old tractors, other implements and even dilapidated trucks. Each time I spot one of these large, landscaped arrangements from the road, or a magnificent piece of welded art, my admiration rises for the creative person who put it all together, and in such an eye-pleasing fashion. In fact, I'm willing to bet my best Carhartt jacket it is the woman of the place who is behind these inventive ideas. This lady might be the alpha farmer, or maybe not, but I see her work-glove-sized prints all over those clever recycling projects.

Only the Lord knows who was the first gal, after the spring snowmelt, to take a clear-eyed look at all the dead iron heaped here and there in her yard, get fed up, and then put her foot down. She not only put it down, but I think that lady put it down hard on the pedal of the nearest Ford pickup with attached flatbed, the one still running. The woman might have dipped into some of her egg money, or earnings from her last game of poker, but she got a move on, and in more ways than one. After reaching town, she rented a forklift, listened closely as the rental guy gave operating instructions, and then hauled her handy-dandy automated helper back home.

If the man of the place wasn't interested in giving a hand, and the teenagers on the premise took one look at their mama and took off, I bet she climbed into the cab of the forklift and got to work. This woman, with the look of purpose in her eye, hefted each pile of rust to where she wanted it. It she couldn't lift it, she made sure John Deere helped her drag it to the designated spot. Once done, and this process most likely took several days, it was time for stage II of Operation Crud Control.

Because it was springtime, and the over-wintered cows were up to their business ends in manure, she had hubby haul and scatter mounds of it around each herd of corralled, rusted pieces of equipment. With some additional bribery, say the promise of a couple of fresh apple pies hit hard with serious piles of vanilla-caramel ice cream, the man felt disposed to work up the ground around the dead metal with a hand-held tiller or a functioning tractor.

Once the cow poop got adequately worked in, it required another trip to town so the woman could stop at the greenhouse to check out the price of quality shrubs and perennials. A frugal lady, one with narrow focus, might take one look at the price tags on those shrubs and plants and slide the Visa card back into her purse. A frugal, but alert and forward-thinking woman, one who had not forgotten what it cost for her male folk to go hunting last fall, would whip her Visa back and forth, like a dude watching a stock car race, while she spent until the flies fell off the wall. It required more bribery and blackmail, but all the plants got into the ground, shovel full by last shovel full.

If the guy involved thought at all, he figured it would have been cheaper and easier to haul the casualties from earlier farm days, whether his or hers, to the land by the creek, out of eyesight, or to the other place several miles away. But what gorgeous results came from the investment of some creative brainpower and hard work! Whether this woman saw the stark beauty in well-built pieces of machinery, or a way to solve the dilemma of dead equipment littered here and there, she turned junk into jewels. After that, the idea took off like a herd of spooked antelope. Another woman saw the results, five light bulbs clicked on in her head, and before you knew it, this sort of landscaping became popular throughout rural America.

But some farm and ranch women are not only thinking of visual beauty, as worthy as it is. These females are shrewd, with an eye to the future. They know a lot of fools all over America have sold off tons of scrap metal to Korea, China or Timbuktu. These smart gals do spend time looking at the cost of a cow-calf pair, and the current price of a bushel of wheat, but they also keep an eye on what scrap metal goes for on the world markets. The ladies with working noggins know there may come a day when it is time to take all that deceased metal sitting in the center of all those hot-looking flowerbeds and turn each piece into cold cash. To these gals, the flowerbeds are like gigantic safe deposit boxes. Admit it. They are smart. Each one keeps those wrecks until the price is right, while ensuring the home place doesn't look like an explosion in a 1950s John Deere factory now gone to rust and ruin.

By this time, the man of the place may have figured out his wife is the cleverer of their two. If he has any sense at all, when the time comes he will arrange for someone to pick up the now-high-priced metal. As a show of good faith, he will offer to take the flatbed truck out to the backside of the country and haul in a load of good-sized, unusually shaped rocks so she can fill the now-vacant spots in those flowerbeds. If those aren't viable options, he can promise to build her one arbor, or maybe five.

If this is you, buddy, words to the wise. You better keep ahead of the lady, because with all those empty spots in the flowerbeds and a fistful of gold certificates earned from the sale of her earlier scrap-iron collection, she might feel the urge to haul home more interesting-looking pieces of decaying machinery. If you are partner to one of these women, brand in your brain the fact that her game is "Buy and Hold, Then Fold," till death do you two part.

Range Wars

Cowboy and Oreo, two border collies, glared at one another as each pulled on his end of a two-foot piece of frayed, dirty rope. Shrewd, conniving and intelligent, they had been at this tug of war for the best part of an hour. Neither one gave any sign of giving in.

"They did that all winter," someone at the dinner table commented.

Although the two dogs are pals, there is a constant struggle for supremacy. Oreo considers himself the alpha dog, and this almost vexes the tail off poor Cowboy, especially when the challenge occurs on his home turf. If they are not sparring over a piece of rope or a toy ball, the dogs use their endless energy to see who will rule the corral, open yard or bed of a truck.

Like everywhere else in the world, there is a lot of bickering among critters in eastern Montana.

The range wars of yesteryear, when sheepherders and cowpokes shot it out over who had rights to what land, are now subdued into some sense of civility. Yet war on the range still happens, make no mistake. Cussing and fighting over land, food and water are natural among the wildlife, whether they have two feet or four feet or slither on the ground.

Crows and squirrels peck and screech over who owns what part of the tree. Wads of cat fur scattered here and there let folks know the neighborhood felines are duking it out over mouse-hunting territory, or the right to poop near the peonies. Beef animals, simple creatures that they are, will head-butt each other to restore territorial rights.

"Even horses have their ways to establish their place," Wayne noted.

Then there are the prairie dogs. Some out-of-state tourists think they are cute little things, but the furry demons from Hades tunnel all over a field or open range, using it for their brand of hibernating, propagating and other abominating practices. The consequence is anything with legs longer than one inch cannot safely travel through the destroyed land without risk of breaking a leg or a neck.

Back and forth, forth and back it goes. The squirrels get the upper hand over the crows, but only until one of them figures out a new strategy to carry on the fight. Cows and horses have deployed teeth, legs and skulls as weapons since creation. Dogs chase cats up trees, and while that goes on, wily raccoons help themselves to the pet food dish. As a matter of fact, raccoons will help themselves to whatever their little hands latch onto, I have noticed.

Prairie dogs get blasted to kingdom come during organized hunts, but only until PETA or some government agency thinks they need to be protected. But these little thugs are so prolific, before long desperate humans get back to blasting them to kingdom come and phooey to what the outsiders think.

All this conflict is natural, but it also spices up life a bit. Imagine if creatures always did the right thing, always got along?

For starters, horses would keep their teeth, feet and heads to themselves. Beef could chest bump and then chew their cuds, or peacefully chew on something else. Cats would poop in the same hole all their lives, and prairie dogs would practice birth control and decide to live in trees. Birds, squirrels, and raccoons would quit their thieving ways. Instead, the little twerps would develop amongst themselves some sort of food co-op.

How boring.

No, it's better if things are left as they are, with all the fighting and cussing. Let the range wars, so to speak, continue.

Oreo might be the alpha dog, but Cowboy evens it up every so often. At a branding a few years ago, one of the relatives set out a jug of water meant to fill the two dogs' water dish. Like a shot, Cowboy moved in and with a swift stream of urine marked the jug as his territory, then trotted off.

Matter settled, for the moment at least.

Since I wrote this story, both Cowboy and Oreo finished their tasks, completed their lives and fulfilled their purposes on this earth. Well done, you two good and faithful servants to man.

Of Mice and Men

At first glance, Montana bachelors might seem ordinary enough people, but I have discovered some of them possess peculiar ways of dealing with certain irritations. Take, for instance, the insidious habits of the ordinary mouse. For a person, especially a bachelor, the ability to get the best of those pernicious little rodents intent on taking over the insides of one's home might prove a difficult matter. A bachelor might face down ornery cows or customers all day. He might plow his fields, acre by grueling acre, without visibly caving in. Not a weak man among them, bachelors are a hardy lot, thinking nothing of living out their days in weather ranging from -10 degrees to 105 degrees and higher. These men are resourceful souls. Being single and having to cook and clean up after themselves, if only once in awhile, makes them that way. Here are some mouse stories people shared with me, tales about the ongoing skirmishes between mice and men.

It seems there were two bachelors who acquired a trailer, but they discovered it was mouse infested. To retaliate, or to maybe just to survive, the men built their version of a mousetrap. They took a goodly bunch of books (Louis L'Amour is a favorite in this part of the country) and stacked them up to make a maze in the living room. While the buddies watched TV, a favorite winter sport, they would be on the lookout for mice. When the furry little poopers came out of their hidey-holes, the critters found themselves running through the maze while the guys picked them off with their BB guns. I suppose it took care of the mice, but if the next owner found the trailer free of mice, chances are good he or she pondered why BB shot peppered the floor.

Mice are warm-blooded animals. When it comes autumn, and colder weather, they look for places to winter in warmth and comfort, like the inside of a barn, garage or best yet, a convenient house. Sometimes the local variety of the genus *Mus* venture too far indoors for his/her comfort and safety.

One morning another young bachelor farmer put some bread in his toaster. As he shoved down the lever that lowers the bread into the heating slots, the lever stuck. Puzzled, but for only a moment because this was his grandma's old toaster and the lever had been know to be persnickety, he gave it another good shove or two. The lever finally made it to the bottom of the slot. As the toaster heated up, the man sniffed the air. "Gee," he thought, "something smells like burned fur." The bread popped up. Being a hungry man and knowing the day lay full ahead, he ate his breakfast, including the toast. Still curious about the odd smell, he peered into the slots of the toaster. Inside one of them lay a very dead, and very singed mouse. That is one mouse that found not only a toasty home, but also an electrically heated coffin.

Duct tape is a marvelous invention. It can be used in so many ways, especially by a frustrated bachelor trying to outwit his mice.

A family member who's a bachelor visited another bachelor friend. When my relative came into the living room, he noticed the old guy's TV completely mummy-wrapped in duct tape, except for the screen and the dials. With miles more tape, the elderly gentleman also had anchored his TV to the wall.

"Why do you have the TV taped to the wall," my curious relative inquired.

"Aw," replied the old man, "the mice get inside the TV, so I taped it to the wall to keep the mice out." A body must admit the old coot exercised some ingenuity, if nothing else.

Why do mice have the upper hand over too many bachelors? Is it because these burly men, after a hard day's work, are just too exhausted to deal with the pooping and urinating little bits of evil? Have mice duped men into accepting the situation as is? If so, I have one solution, but it won't be cheap.

A good mouser cat might help, but what a mice-infested bachelor pad needs is a woman. I didn't say "wife," or "girlfriend," but a female hired to deal with the problem. OK, I just mentioned the four-letter word to a lot of thrifty bachelors. To "hire" means to put real money on the table, something some single men try to avoid. Why not hire a woman? All it would take is one or two ladies experienced with waging war on the rodents. One woman with murder in her eye, fire in her belly and armed with poison, traps and a long-handled broom, would do the Russian mafia proud. If all else fails, scour the countryside for a female who served in the military or uses firearms and likes to hunt, because a woman tends to have more finesse in matters of guns and death. She will bring something effective, like her .45 or a little but lethal pistol. Armed with heat, when the woman is finished with the mice, the guy will not only have a rodent-free house, he will hold new respect for the female's ability to use small-arms firepower. An added bonus, if a man looks at it in the right way, his house will now sport a neat and interesting series of vents.

But bachelor, after all is said, done and paid for, don't be stupid and ask the woman to clean up the blood, guts and tails, especially if she's still holding mama's little helper. Your final goal is to survive this business proposition. Face up to the truth. The payer's part of this deal is to police the shells and mop up the guts, fur and blood. If you parked the bucket and mop nearby, hoping she'd offer to help, more the fool you look. Keep mouth shut, and start working the mop and bucket before she decides to empty another magazine right then and there.

Hang Onto Your Hat

In eastern Montana, a cowboy hat is standard gear for most people who spend a lot of time farming, working cattle or just being outside. It protects the wearer's head from the summer's roast-the-eyeballs heat, and from the deep freeze of winter. In fact, a good hat is more valuable to a hardworking Montanan than urban people might realize. But a quality hat is often hard to find. Just ask hat maker Ken Hess.

Years ago, I met the gentleman in Miles City, found out he grew up in Fallon and loved to tell stories. Hess creates handmade cowboy hats, each one as smooth as velvet, and has done so for years.

"It takes me between five and eight hours to build a hat," Hess said. "I try to build a hat a day." Hess and his wife, Vicki, own Kickin' Ass Hat Company on Main Street in Miles, as the locals call the town. Hess may be the only hat maker in the history of the city.

The native Montanan explains his occupation.

"I was born good-looking instead of rich," he said. "Since I couldn't afford to buy good-quality cowboy hats, I decided to learn how to make them."

Hess studied the art of making cowboy hats with another custom hatter. He worked with his mentor for nearly six months and started making hats on his own in 1999. Hess tells people one thing right off and up front.

"There are places you go that make hats, but they don't do them by hand. You have to get to know the hat, and that doesn't happen if folks take shortcuts or have fancy machines do a lot of the work. By the time I'm done, I know each hat inside and out."

Hess thinks hats have personalities. Some are easy to work with, others are stubborn, and some are so ornery he throws them into the garbage can. Whether easy or stubborn, it's a labor-intensive job.

The making of a good cowboy hat starts with a blank, which is nothing more than a plain, unshaped hat. Hess only works with the highest quality beaver-felt blanks. He selects a suitable blank and pulls it down over an antique wooden hat block. The blank often balks during this stretching process, so Hess uses wooden slats, called pulls, to push the crown of the blank all the way to the bottom of the block.

Then Hess ropes the blank, the unshaped hat. He pulls a heavy cord down over the brim and anchors the cord where the crown and brim meet. The blank, now settled down, is ready for the blocking process. The purpose of blocking is to rid the blank of all wrinkles, and Hess has the perfect tool for this.

"I have an expensive, high-tech steamer," he said. "Actually, I got the steam iron at the pawn shop for a dollar. It's lasted me eight years, so far." All wrinkles in the felt must be steamed out from both the crown and the brim. This process takes at least 30 minutes.

The wrinkle-free blank is now ready to sand. Hess removes any nubs or bumps during the sanding process. He is particular about this and won't go on to the next step until the blank is as smooth as velvet.

Cowboy hats have a distinctive shape. Some hats are rounded at the crown or the top. Other hats sport an indented crown. With both hat shapes, rounded or indented, Hess works the brim of each hat so both sides of the brim are curved upward and in a forward point. These curves not only give the hat style but also serve as troughs to channel moisture landing on the hat, such as in a rainstorm, off it and onto the ground.

Hess uses both steam and hand manipulation to mold the blank into its distinctive shape.

A steamer heats and lightly moistens the felt. Hess then shapes the blank with his hands until it looks just right. The shaped blank is set aside to cool. He continues shaping it as necessary throughout the building process. While the blank cools, Hess gets out his needle and thread. Every respectable cowboy hat has a sweatband and he doesn't stint here, either.

"I use goatskin because it's the best you can get." Hess sews the sweatband using bonded nylon thread. He'll mark the blank by printing its size, his name and the date inside each sweatband.

The hatband can be the most distinctive part of the hat.

"You can have whatever you want for a hatband," Hess said. Many folks like a plain fabric band, but more than one lady or gent prefers elaborately braided cord, called hitching. This, too, is sewn on by hand.

The lining for the hat, which Hess purchases already finished, is sewn in once the hatband is in place. He uses linings made from fabric containing silk and other types of fiber. Most customers choose a white lining, but they also come in other colors.

Hess sews on the binding once the blank is lined. Binding, which is applied at the outer edge of the brim, can be whatever the customer wants, including rawhide. Hess uses grosgrain, a tightly woven tape, for binding most hats, and he uses a sewing machine for this step.

"My wife taught me how to use the sewing machine. They wouldn't let me take sewing in high school."

The once shapeless blank is now a real hat.

Hess is proud of his one-of-a-kind cowboy hats. Although he makes them to sell off the rack, many are custom made.

Who would buy a cowboy hat? Lots of people.

"I've sold hats to cowboys, bishops and lawyers," he said, "and I've sold hats to people living all over the world."

Every cowboy hat needs proper care to last the lifetime of its owner, and Hess has a few tips so people will do right by their hats.

"Keep it out of the heat. I've seen people ruin a brand-spanking-new hat. They lay it on the backseat of a car, hop onto a plane and go somewhere. When they come back, the hat's shrunk."

He cautions owners to groom it with a regular household brush that has medium-stiff nylon bristles.

"The best way to store a hat, when it's not on your head, is to hang it on something," he added.

For those who wear a genuine cowboy hat, whether for business or pleasure, Hess has three pieces of folklore to share:

(a.) A wise man or woman always sets his or her cowboy hat upside down, on its crown, so the luck doesn't fall out of it.
(b.) Keep in mind to never pick a hat up off the bed and then put it on your head. Always knock it on the floor first.

(c.) Most important, never mess with another person's hat. It will save a lot of pain if you keep your hands to yourself.

Hess, after all these years, still keeps busy building new hats and also renovates ones that have a few miles on them. He cannot make an old hat look brand new, but he can give it another chance in the ring.

Renovation includes cleaning the soiled hat, putting in a new sweatband and liner and replacing the hatband, if needed. He won't use chemicals to clean hats because he feels they are too dangerous.

"I'd rather stick around and enjoy my family than die cleaning some greasy old hat with chemicals," he said.

A high-quality hat doesn't come cheap, and Hess is upfront about that.

"My new hats range from a few hundred dollars, on up," he said.

Hess knows a person is defined by his or her cowboy hat and he will do his best to make sure all his customers hang onto their hats, one way or the other.

"I had a friend die in an accident," Hess said. "I cleaned the blood off his hat and he wore it to his funeral. I also gave the eulogy."

Virginia A. Johnson

These days, Ken and his wife spend part of each year, November through March, in Wickenburg, Arizona. Wickenburg is about 50 miles north of Phoenix.

While in Wickenburg, Ken carries on his business of creating custom-made hats. The rest of the year a person will find him in Miles City, still building those hats.

Butchering Chickens

In the good old days it wasn't a simple task to prepare a crisp, hot and mouth-watering platter of fried chicken. Most of the time, this responsibility fell to the woman of the house. Armed with an ax or hatchet, she did the foul deed to the unsuspecting fowl blissfully pecking in the barnyard. The day of the dinner she rose early, caught the doomed bird, killed, plucked, cleaned and cooled it. If this happened on a Sunday, and after the meal preparations were under control, she might put on her bonnet or hat and head to church.

A number of years ago, when my elderly Aunt Pauline lived three doors down from us in Fallon, I talked to her about butchering chickens. She had been in failing health, and I worried about her. How could I pull her out of the world of silence she now inhabited? This story is of the time I prodded her to share with me how to properly butcher a chicken for Sunday dinner.

"While you are in Terry," I told Wayne, "stop by the little grocery store and buy a whole chicken." The plump, juicy bird would serve as a nice variation from the usual beef. Aunt Pauline might like the change, too.

Pauline Kalmback Gaub, born in 1915, grew up in eastern Montana. Her mother and father, like thousands of other Germans-from-Russia people, immigrated to the United States at the turn of the 20th century. Tiny as a pullet, Pauline looked as lean and sparse as a lone tree scrapping for life on an otherwise barren hillside. Frugal, tidy and industrious, she moved through life with purpose. She spent her childhood and young womanhood on her parents' farm. After marriage to Uncle Henry, my mother's younger brother, Pauline worked hard as a rancher's wife for more than half a century.

During my childhood, I saw Pauline only a few times, yet I always felt welcome in her home. She served simple but hearty meals. Even more important to a kid with a sweet tooth, her kitchen counter kept at least one dessert at the ready, and her freezer was full of goodies waiting to meet their culinary destiny.

After Uncle Henry's death, Pauline's sense of purpose evaporated. Worse, macular degeneration now clouded her world. When our conversation about chickens took place, her once-busy kitchen seemed to grieve as well. The cookie sheets and roasting pans had been put out to pasture; the electric stove a now-unused testimony to what had been. Although she could walk, Pauline spent most of her days sitting in a chair, staring into space, and seldom talking. Not accustomed to this out-of-character inactivity, I worried.

And I had a supper to get on the table too.

"This is all they had," Wayne said. He plunked down a whole, frozen chicken. I picked it up. Its yellow tinge warned me this was no spring chicken when it met its end.

"Arkansas! Couldn't you find a fresh chicken?"

"That's all they had."

"I cannot feed this aging bird to the relatives," I mumbled. Pauline might not see, but her taste buds worked just fine. She would know it wasn't a fresh bird by its smell alone.

So there it was. The over-the-hill hen pecked away at the prospects for a decent evening meal.

And I still fussed about Pauline.

I stared at the poor excuse of a fowl for some time. I also sent a prayer heavenward. What could I do with a chicken whose origins I dared not divulge to Aunt Pauline? While I am at it, Lord, how can I rouse her mind, if only for a little while?

Pauline. Chickens.

Aha! With pencil and notebook in hand, I trotted to her home. Maybe a conversation about butchering chickens would wake the elderly woman from her mental slumber. Not my favorite topic to chat about, I admitted, but it deserved a try.

"Aunt Pauline, tell me about when you butchered chickens."

My request visibly startled her. Good. Would she come out of her self-imposed silence? Although she had butchered chickens for over half a century, my initial comment didn't bring forth any words. It looked like Pauline needed an additional peck to get her moving.

"When, during the year, did you usually butcher chickens?" I asked. She looked in my direction, trying hard to see my face. Her face always intrigued me. I wondered if the genes from a long-dead ancestor, rooted in the East, had found their outlet in Pauline's high cheekbones and beautiful, upturned eyes. Although ravaged by disease, those eyes still held charm.

"We usually did fryers in the summer." Pauline paused, as though remembering. "I killed one or two chickens each Sunday morning. We would have them for Sunday dinner." Once she pulled forth those sentences from somewhere deep inside her mind, we were off and trotting through past memories of how to catch, kill, clean and cook the centerpiece of a traditional rural Sunday dinner.

"I grabbed the chicken. Do it while it is still sitting in the coop," she advised me. I could almost see Pauline's small, strong hands snatch the unfortunate bird off its perch. "If you chase a chicken around the yard and then catch it, it won't bleed well."

"Would a chicken get suspicious and squawk? I asked

"It would squawk, but I held it by its bill so it couldn't squawk no more. I put the chicken's head on a wooden block and chopped it off. Then I held it until it quit jumping and fluttering. Otherwise it would flop around in the dirt."

Pauline moved on with her plain, no-nonsense instructions about removing the feathers of the ill-fated fowl.

"I dipped it in hot water." Her voice took on an edge of concern. "Don't use too hot a water or the skin will come off with the feathers." Her fine-boned face, wrinkled with time and tanned by decades working in the sun, wore an expression appropriate to our serious conversation.

Once the bird was plucked, Pauline used fire to singe off the hair of the chicken.

"Chickens had hair?" I asked, surprised. She nodded.

"In the fall of the year, the old chickens were really loaded with them," she replied.

Pauline would pour a small amount of rubbing alcohol in a dish and set the alcohol on fire. Turning the chicken around and around, she singed the entire body of the bird, then chopped off its feet.

After washing the chicken in cold water, she gutted it.

"You get the crop out first by opening up the neck and pulling it out." Although unsure about the location of a chicken's crop, I kept quiet. "Then you cut open the stomach and pull out the intestines."

After gutting the bird, my aunt cut off the tail and cleaned the carcass of all blood. I did not ask what she did with the head, tail, feet and innards. She might not remember, and I didn't care to know.

"You wash it in cold water again, and keep it in cold water until it is time to cut up the chicken, dip it in flour and salt, and fry it for dinner."

In the early days on the farm at Cabin Creek, Aunt Pauline cooked on a cast-iron stove. Fuel was either wood or coal. Many years earlier, my maternal grandmother, Christina Gaub, hand-built a summer kitchen, using stones from the nearby creek. It was separate from the house. Whether Pauline used this kitchen or prepared food in the old farmhouse, it meant she cooked those summer meals during outside temperatures often hotter than the hinges of Hell, as my father liked to say, along with the additional heat of a blazing hot cookstove.

Pauline told me the wing was her favorite piece of fried chicken.

"I had all my teeth then. Now I like something soft."

"Did the butchering process bother you?" I asked.

"Yes, sometimes it bothered me."

At this point, Pauline looked tired so we took a break. When we picked up the conversation later on, she had more to say. Aha, another good sign.

"I forgot to tell you," she said. "When you take out the insides, you have to cut out the gizzard and liver and save them. But you will see that." Her face suddenly registered a surprised look, and then she laughed as though realizing she had said something amusing. The skin at the outside edges of her eyes crinkled up tight. "I know you ain't going to butcher no chickens, but I forgot to tell you that part." She ended her verbal instructions with a smile in my direction. I left my now-alert aunt sitting in her chair. It was time to deal with the problem of dinner.

Yet something had changed between us as we talked. Unknowing, I had given Pauline the opportunity to share part of her past with a family member, someone interested in what she had to say. She gave me a gift as well. I came away from our conversations with a new appreciation of how a tough, resourceful woman lived on the Montana prairie. I admired her. In those early years of marriage, Pauline learned how to conquer life on an isolated farm, one with no running water, only a small stone cistern. Electricity came in later on. In these conditions, my sturdy aunt developed skills for survival, tools useful for her entire life. Our visit gave me much to think about, and a solution to my supper problem.

I chickened out.

The Arkansas bird never made it to the table that night. I served pork chops instead.

Pauline Kalmback Gaub went to be with her Lord Jesus Christ on March 26, 2017. She would have celebrated her 102 birthday on October 22, 2017.

Rest in Jesus, Aunt Pauline.

Solitary Warriors

The man kept his eyes straight ahead as he stared at something I could not see. When conscious of my presence, he turned his face in my direction. Once the man noticed I wore no nametag, or no sign of rank, his face and his eyes moved back to that object, invisible to me but known to him.

Walking on, I noticed men stationed at various positions within the room and down the hall. Some glanced my way, others ignored me as they attacked their assigned task. All had one thing in common. They were warriors.

At some point in their lives, each had served in some branch of the United States military. Most of these men experienced combat at one time or another. They knew how life went in the military, and bits of those memories, like tarnished brass buttons on a moth-eaten wool uniform, stayed with them. These warriors, however, did not live in a military barracks. Soldiers once, they now resided in a nursing home for incapacitated veterans in Glendive, Montana.

I had come to the facility to see my first cousin, Reuben. Now in his mid-80s, he served in the Army during World War II. The fact of his military service is significant, as our grandparents were lifelong pacifists. No one in the extended family told me of Grandmother Gaub's thoughts of Reuben's part in the war. It is doubtful she approved.

Reuben, along with his unit, arrived in Germany toward the end of the conflict. The men experienced some combat, he told me, but they spent the bulk of their time as part of the occupation forces.

An eastern Montana boy and built spare, Reuben grew up used to hard work. If America hadn't had those thousands of farm boys like Reuben, and girls too, youngsters accustomed to harsh conditions and long hours of demanding labor, I doubt the United States could have maintained the tenacious strength needed to win that war.

I do not enjoy visiting nursing homes, regardless of how nice the environment, or how caring the staff. Unlike my daughter, a doctor who served with the Army in Afghanistan, I have no experience caring for wounded men, young or old. And these men in Glendive? They are frail, often wheelchair bound and incontinent. Worse, each one is incarcerated in a body bent on betrayal.

Reuben is in the advanced stages of Parkinson's disease. I dreaded a visit to him because I felt helpless.

I longed to see the Reuben I remembered as a kid.

Back then he was a quiet, good-looking man with a slow smile and a gentle sense of humor. I rarely saw him during my childhood. But during our early years in Fallon, I discovered he made delicious fruit pies. Reuben loved to bring them, along with Vivian, his pretty wife of nearly 50 years, to our family get-togethers. Since then, Vivian had passed away and Reuben, in the inescapable grip of a disease that destroyed his mother and sister, now lived in the veteran's home.

"Hello Reuben, " I greeted my cousin. Although busy with breakfast, he looked up at me. At first he seemed confused, but once his mind sorted me out, a big smile spread across his face. I tried not to look at another man at the table as he did hand-to-hand combat with his breakfast. A third man at the table stood up.

"Well, well, we have company," he said. "Would you like a cup of coffee?" The older gentleman introduced himself as Steve and kept talking to me while the others worked on their pancakes. At first I thought he was one of the attendants but soon realized this hospitable man was a resident.

Without warning, a man at another table let out a loud and blistering stream of cuss words. Startled and uncomfortable, I told Reuben, "Perhaps I should come back another time."

"No, you must stay and visit with Reuben," Steve replied. His face revealed a mixture of concern and perhaps slight embarrassment. "You cannot leave him. Not yet."

I stayed.

While we chatted, Steve oversaw the needs at the table, serving as sentinel for this little band of men while they carried out their morning duties. He made sure nothing upset the group or took them by surprise.

After breakfast, my husband wheeled Reuben to his room. Steve walked there also and we visited along the way. Emboldened by our conversation, I asked this stranger if he cared to pray with me. He told me he was a Roman Catholic. I told him I was a Protestant. Despite a vast canyon between our ages and our faiths, and in the hallway of a nursing home, for a moment or two our souls joined in communion with God.

Back in Reuben's room, my cousin and I talked of family and other everyday bits of gossip about our shared relatives. His voice did not carry above a whisper, and he easily tired, but Reuben sat up straight and looked me in the eye. I hoped he couldn't sense my reluctance and discomfort, at least on this day. With growing courage, I asked Reuben if he would like me to pray for him. He nodded. Afterward, he seemed pleased. And during our prayer, I realized something of great value.

Reuben, as well as Steve and the other men, were *still* warriors. They lived in a military company of sorts and they followed the orders of those who cared for them. Each one stayed engaged in warfare as they fought against disease, disablement and death. The men battled on with both their hearts and their souls.

That man at another table during breakfast, the one who startled me with his blistering cuss words? Perhaps his mind, lost in a swirling confusion of dementia, knew no better. Or it might have been his only weapon to combat an enemy intent on destroying him.

Each of these men deserves all the dignity and sense of self-worth we can give them. Just as these soldiers, many years earlier, carried out their military duties, now it is our duty to be mindful of them. They are solitary warriors, bivouacked in a place they never wanted to be, and we must never forget them or leave them behind. I will visit Reuben again, and when I do, I will carry myself with dignity and pride at what my cousin did for his country and for all of us. Until then, I have one prayer for him and for each of his fellow warriors.

Fight on.

A Greenhorn Gal

God relieved Reuben Schock of duty on this Earth on Aug. 6, 2011, at the Eastern Montana Veteran's Home in Glendive. Reuben's family was with him at the time of his death.

Prairie Roses

The small, spindly rose bush did not look worth saving. Stunted from years of little moisture and long neglected, it displayed a puny collection of withered leaves. Thick, sharp thorns covered its tough, woody stalks. The plant had survived for decades on the east side of the old, vacant house in Fallon. Despite its pitiful condition, I decided the rose deserved another chance. I weeded around the base of the plant, bedded it down with cow manure and headed back to Oregon for the winter.

The following June, the little bush produced dozens of bright yellow blooms. Each one had five to seven petals, and each flower let off a soft scent. Was this yellow rose native to eastern Montana? If not, how did it get to this part of the United States? After some time elapsed, and one failed attempt at a transplant, I realized it was time to learn more about this tenacious, tough rose and how to care for it.

The Harison's Yellow Rose, as it is called, is not native to Montana. The hybrid seedling rose originated in the early 19th century at the home of George F. Harison, an attorney in New York. It is often called the Oregon Trail Rose, or the Yellow Rose of Texas. Perhaps someone journeying to the Oregon Country shared slips with a Montana homesteader. Or maybe a cowboy, coming home from a cattle drive to Texas, brought back a cutting. How the rose found its way to my little piece of Montana will remain a mystery. One thing is certain. The scrawny bush clung tight to life despite the unmerciful cycles of weather common to this part of the state.

I found there are four species of wild bush roses growing in the state. They are the Prickly rose, the Prairie rose, the Nootka rose and the Woods' rose. One, the Prickly rose, is considered an endangered plant. Wild Montana roses, along with the Harison, are tough plants indeed. They learn to adapt despite human neglect and those natural elements of the land bent on grinding down and destroying anything weak. They live, bear fruit and, if given a decent opportunity, will spread their roots and grow big. For me, a wild rose reminds me of the Montana women who have walked through my life.

Whether transplanted from somewhere else or from rootstock with a long Montana history, these women, with their adaptability and resilience, are a marvel.

I recollect the elderly woman I interviewed for our daily newspaper in Albany, Oregon, more than a decade ago. From England, she came to eastern Montana as a young, somewhat idealistic WWII war bride. Her first book, an autobiography, proved so honest, stark and brutal, I could not finish reading it. This woman thrived despite human cruelty and a withering climate. To me, her outgoing personality seemed like a bouquet of bright red roses, ready to warm my heart. In her late 80s at the time of our interview, she busied herself with work on a second book, anxious to get it done before her time on Earth stopped forever.

The maid who serviced our hotel room in Bozeman looked too young and too frail to be doing such work. As I looked into her face, I saw both vulnerability and a weariness of soul. When she found out we lived in the tiny community of Crabtree, Oregon, her eyes lit up.

"I spent my 21st birthday at the Crabtree tavern," she happily recalled.

My stomach tightened. Many locals considered the tavern a rough place. There have been at least two murders at the tavern during our life in the rural community. I gave her a tip, my largest ever. I prayed she used it for food, not alcohol or drugs. When she saw the large bill, her face broke into a beautiful smile. I knew I would never see her again, and I worried. Would she survive? She seemed fragile, but then what did I know? Some roses are tougher than they appear. As we drove east, her face rode with me into the cold day ahead.

During our meal in the restaurant of a hotel in Portland, we mentioned to the server our home in eastern Montana. Within minutes, another woman server, probably in late middle age, walked briskly to our table. Was it true we lived in Montana?

Yes indeed. We told her of our house in Fallon, how often we traveled there and so forth. She shared with us about her years growing up in her home state, and I sensed her longing to go back. She looked resilient, like someone who weathered more than one cold snap or parched summer. She would find her way back, I told myself, if not soon, then someday. If not tucked into the saddlebag of someone else's life, then on her own.

The hands of my heart are not big enough to gather in all the women I have met whose souls were shaped by their years in Montana. Many I count as friends, some are casual acquaintances and others merely passed a few of their life's moments in my presence. The rest? They are part of my maternal bloodline, part of my roots.

I think of my mother, grandmother, aunts and female cousins. Some were tough to begin with, and some grew to be tough. Sadly, a few could not withstand the harsh elements of life. Those women were the endangered roses in our family. They survived, but like my neglected Harison, had difficulty thriving as the years progressed.

The young women within my extended family, including my daughters and youngest granddaughter, are the next generations of new shoots sprouted from roots planted in Montana soil more than a hundred years earlier. Some are still Montanans; others have put down roots elsewhere. Nonetheless, it is their turn to learn how to withstand the elements present in their lives. I pray each one, like our common ancestors, Joseph and Christina Gaub, fully include Christ in her life and like the Harison rose, not only thrive, but enrich *her* extended family and her part of the world.

I transplanted one of the straggly bushes of my yellow rose from Aunt Christina's place to our other house in Fallon during the cold, miserably wet spring of 2011. I gave it the protection of a building, and in a spot graced by the morning sun. The spindly bush received little babying, but I did make sure it got fertilizer and a light pruning. A neighbor kept the rose watered during the hot months of summer. When we came back the first of September, the bush looked healthy and happy in its new location. Someday a piece of the rootstock will travel back to Oregon with me. When it does, and if it survives, someone is bound to exclaim, "Where did you find a start of the old Oregon Trail Rose?"

I will correct that individual.

"What you see is a yellow Harison, and yes, people might call it the Oregon Trail Rose, but this one, with its sharp thorns and beautiful old-fashioned blooms, I call my Montana prairie rose."

Part II

Soul Good Food

Early Montanans, like all settlers throughout America, lived off the land. These men and women learned to create edible meals from ordinary staples like flour, lard, salt, a few root vegetables and, if lucky, a piece of meat. In the past, generations of Americans lived by the rule: "Eat what's on your plate." They had to, or it meant starve with their boots on.

"If you are hungry enough, you will eat anything," Mom told me the one time I turned up my nose at some dish featured on the dinner table. She spoke from experience. Food was not easy to come by during her growing up years at Cabin Creek. Because she held this practical point of view and I adapted to it, Mom's meals, however modest, tasted good to me.

Come autumn, she prepared certain special dishes. Imagine forking into a plump, steaming-hot German rice roll on a cold and rainy Saturday. With each bite, one's mouth filled with the mingled flavors of spicy sausage, hamburger and rice. Then there were cinnamon-dusted pumpkin blossoms, still warm from the oven. During fall, if Mom spent the day outside "putting the yard to bed for winter," the blossoms became our supper along with a big glass of milk. Winter meant hearty soups, stews, pot roast and stewed chicken with dumplings. In early spring, she served as least one large bowl of handpicked tender dandelion greens, wilted with bacon fat, spritzed with vinegar, then crowned with bits of crisp fried bacon and chopped boiled egg. We celebrated summertime with her open-skillet fried chicken, accompanied by a salad of boiled, diced potatoes lolling, like fat, decadent Romans, in a bowl thick with creamy mayonnaise and chopped boiled eggs. And on it went. My mother, like thousands of other women who lived as adults during the Great Depression, beat back the difficult times in life by serving comfort foods, "soul foods," made with the basics and with love.

I believe heirloom family recipes are valuable documents. Each one enlightens me as to what foods the individual cook used during a certain period in history, a peek at local customs of that time and sometimes of the turmoil going on in the world. As my years living in Montana unfolded, I gained access to recipes unique to our extended family. They might not always be dishes Mom prepared, but each culinary offering gave me a more complete picture of that person and his or her ethnic history.

How does a person describe cousin Shirley's knipfla? A miniature dumpling, knipfla are bits of dough steamed in a savory broth, spooned hot from the cooking pot, then nuzzled next to boiled-tender potatoes and butter-fried toasty bread cubes. But knipfla did not begin with Shirley. The recipe came from her mother, Pauline, who learned it from her mother, and so its lineage goes both back both in time and to another world.

What about kuchen? How many ways could a thrifty German or Scandinavian farm wife prepare this basic sweet-dough coffee cake? Kuchen's origins might be traced to the Old World, but an immigrant woman or man brought his or her family's version to America and adapted it. No stick of rhubarb, bucket of chokecherries or handful of raisins was safe come baking time. Desserts like these, both economical and tasty, filled up the bread-basket of a hungry kid, farmer or bachelor and made life more enjoyable too. It might be simple eating but it meant soul-good food to many.

This book does not feature many extended-family recipes. At this point, my collection is small but growing. I do include goodies from my files, recipes passed on by other special people in my life. Each one, tinkered with, became mine. Handed-down recipes are like wind-driven tumbleweeds, meandering here and there from person to person. As a result, at times the authorship of the recipe is lost. I apologize.

Each recipe, and you may recognize many, is relatively easy to make. I believe a well-used recipe carries with it a story or explanation, so I include these anecdotes as well. I also include some general alternatives for the person preparing meals for someone with dietary restrictions such as low-sodium, dairy-free or gluten free.

My family is like your family. We eat to stay alive and to stay healthy. Sometimes the need to satisfy a food hunger, as it gnaws deep within oneself, rises to the surface. These are times you and I crave more than an everyday experience in eating. Perhaps this longing comes from a desire to connect with the good people and the pleasant times and places experienced during childhood. Often a specific food or a treasured recipe ignites memories of that place, that time and those people. I cannot relive the past and neither can you, but when we have the chance to eat the unique dish or reread the old recipe, memories open wide. We connect once again to those people and that past. If that happens, a part of my soul dances, and perhaps yours does too, with a deep and extravagant joy.

Saddle-Broke Pot Roast

On a chilly autumn or winter day, a savory pot roast of beef cooking in the oven or an electric slow cooker produces a most hospitable aroma. Its mouth-tingling smell, along with onions, garlic and spices, transforms a cold house into a warm, cozy home. It is safe to say a tender, rich and juicy roast is one of many Americans' soul foods.

This method of preparing a less-expensive cut of beef is popular especially in lean financial times. When people cannot afford the better cuts off the animal but desire something besides chicken or meatloaf as the centerpiece to a Sunday dinner or other special meal, bring on the pot roast. My mother served it as one of her favorite meat offerings to our family.

Pot roast is easy to prepare if the chef remembers one principle: A tougher cut of beef, such as chuck, must be slow-cooked in a small amount of liquid. This method of cooking meat is called braising. During the process, the liquid in the pot must not be allowed to evaporate because moist heat breaks down the structure of the tough muscles, making the cut tender and full of flavor. With that rule in mind, always cover the cooking pot with a tight-fitting lid or several layers of tin foil. Braising a tougher cut of meat is the perfect means of cooking the two legs of the cow going through the gate first.

There are two ways to prepare a cut of chuck roast: Straight and simple, or all dolled up. A cautionary note: Before you do anything to the roast, observe which way the grain of the meat runs in relation to the shape of the roast. The reason for this will come later.

With the straight-up method, season the cut of beef on each side with pepper and spices. Salt need not be added at this time. Omit dredging it in flour. Brown each side of the roast in a hot, oiled skillet. Place the browned roast in a heavy-gauge, deep-sided pan. Add water or other liquid so the roast sits in ¼ to ½ inch of it. As the meat structures break down, some additional moisture will be released, so don't drown the roast in liquid. For a one-dish meal, accompany the roast with peeled onions, carrots, potatoes or other root vegetables. As mentioned earlier, cover the roast with a tight- fitting lid.

The dolled-up version means dusting all sides of the roast with flour, seasoned with pepper, paprika and other herbs. Some people make thin cuts into the meat, and load each cut with slivers of garlic before rolling it in flour. Brown each side of the roast in a hot, oiled skillet, as mentioned earlier. With both methods, the browning process seals in the juices of the meat. (It is true some research supports the hypothesis the browning of meats creates carcinogens, but each individual must decide the pros and cons on this.) Place the prepared meat in a heavy pan. Add onions, root veggies and liquid. Some people douse the roast with wine, strong coffee or tomato juice. Cover the roast in the same manner mentioned earlier.

Pop the roast into a preheated oven, 325 to 350 degrees. Let the oven do the rest of the work for the next two to three hours or more, depending on the size of the roast. A three-to four-pound roast requires two to three hours. The meat is done when it can be easily cut with a table knife and fork. Once done, remove the roast from the oven. Allow it to sit in the pan, still covered and with its veggie buddies, for at least 15 minutes.

Remove the roast from its pan. Cut the roast, but slice each piece *crosswise* to the grain of the meat. Submerge the slices in their broth or with gravy. Never let the sliced meat set by itself. Always keep it covered or the moisture within the meat will evaporate, causing the strands of cooked beef to tighten up and the roast to be as dry and tough as an old piece of saddle leather.

If dinner will not be for a while, place both the covered meat and the vegetables, also covered, in a 250-degree oven. Serve piping hot.

The following recipe details how cousin Shirley fixes her pot roast, something she served at annual brandings for many years. I call her method "saddle broke" because when she gets through with the meat, it is fall-apart tender. Slabs of her hot, juicy, tender roast beef, squeezed between two layers of a homemade yeast roll, are a nice way to say "Thank you!" to all the workers who come to help on a very important day in the life of a cattle rancher.

POT ROAST RECIPE
Ingredients:

Chuck roast of beef, 2 pounds or larger
1-2 onions, sliced
1-2 C. water (start with lesser amount)
Salt
Pepper

Directions:
(Part One)

Place the roast in a deep-sided roasting pan. Do not brown the sides of the roast beforehand. Salt and pepper to taste. Cover top of roast with sliced onions. Add water and cover roast with two layers of tin foil, wrapped snuggly around the outer edges of the pan. Put the roast in a preheated oven set at 350 degrees. Bake at this temperature for 30 to 60 minutes and then lower the temperature to 325 degrees. Bake until meat is no longer red in the center. Remove from the oven and let it set for 15 minutes.

Place the roast on a cutting board. Slice it into 1/3 to 1/2-inch thick slices. Be sure to cut crosswise to grain of meat. Lay the slices back into the baking pan and arrange them in a fan-shaped pattern so each one partially overlaps the next. Cover most of the meat slices with the broth and onions. Cover the pot with two layers of tin foil. The sliced meat and its juices can be refrigerated for a day, or frozen, until the second stage of preparation.

(Part Two)
When you are ready for the second stage, place the covered pan in a preheated, (300-325 degrees) oven and bake until the meat is saddle-broke and fall-apart tender. Serve slices with their juice. If you freeze the meat first, allow it to thaw in the refrigerator. For pre-frozen or chilled meat, start the second roasting period at a temperature of 350 degrees until the meat is steaming hot, and then reduce the temperature to 300 degrees. Serve hot. Refrigerate any leftovers.

Note: Shirley uses a better quality cut of beef, such as a sirloin tip roast, for this recipe.

Lightning-Quick Yeast Rolls

This recipe for yeast rolls is easy to make; the dough rises quickly and the end product tastes good. People go for them, and that tells me the recipe is a winner.

The best yeast breads and rolls are made with hard, red winter wheat flour, the variety of wheat grown and harvested in central Montana. This type of bread flour develops a different kind of gluten strand, one that will be long and stretchy. These long strands hold up well while the gases, released by the activated yeast, work to push the dough upward and outward. Long gluten strands in the dough give the finished bread and rolls good height.

I buy Wheat Montana© flour each time we pass by Three Forks. I love how it makes beautiful, flavorful yeast rolls and bread. It is sold in most grocery stores throughout Montana.

If you haven't tried this brand of flour, check it out:

Wheat Montana Bakery and Farms
10778 Hwy 287
Three Forks, MT 59752
1.800.535.2798
www.wheatmontana.com

YEAST ROLLS RECIPE
Ingredients:

2 T. dry yeast
2 C. warm milk or warm water
1/4 -1/3 cup sugar
2 eggs
1/3 C. melted butter or vegetable oil
1/2 -1 t. salt
4 C. all-purpose flour
2 C. whole-wheat flour
Extra flour as needed

Directions:
Combine the yeast with the warm milk or water. Add the sugar and stir with a large wooden spoon or electric mixer until the yeast and milk are well blended. I use an electric mixer for the first part of the process. Add the eggs, oil or butter and salt. Beat until all the ingredients are thoroughly mixed, like a milkshake. Add 2 cups of whole-wheat flour and one cup of the all-purpose flour. Beat, with the mixer, until the dough has a smooth consistency. Remove the spoon or mixer.

Add another 2 cups of flour. Knead, by hand, the dough for six to eight minutes, putting in the last cup of flour, more or less, as needed. Do not use too much flour. The dough should be smooth and elastic. Some people say it should be as smooth as a baby's bottom. You get the idea.

Let the dough rise until double in bulk. BEWARE! Do not wander off somewhere. This dough rises fast due to the amount of yeast in ratio to the salt and sugar. If the room is warm, you have around 30 to 60 minutes. That's why I call them Lightning Quick Rolls. After the dough rises, or even if it over-rises, punch it down and go on to the next step.

Shape the dough into rolls (dinner, hamburger, hot dog, etc.). Place them on a lightly greased cookie sheet or other baking pan. Let the rolls rise until **almost** double in bulk. Again, if you do not keep an eye on these little workers, they will get away from you.

Bake the rolls in a preheated 350-degree oven for about 15 minutes or until they are a light golden brown. Remove from the oven and spread butter over the top of the rolls. Cool slightly before serving. One batch makes around two-dozen decent-size dinner rolls. The baked rolls freeze well too.

Full of Beans

In Montana, a big vat of spicy BBQ beans is standard food at a gathering. It is fortunate I had a long history of consuming beans before moving to Fallon.

Mom rarely cooked up a pot of dried beans, but Dad did. His slow-cooker beans tasted good, a minor miracle if one considered my father's odd culinary tastes.

Dad liked to experiment with lots of things, and he enjoyed tinkering with food during the rare times he attempted to prepare a meal for us. One time, when Mom attended a meeting, he made his version of peanut butter gravy, with peanut butter, grease, flour and milk for our supper. My brother and I, sick with some sort of gastro-intestinal bug, not only had to smell it cooking—Dad expected us to chow down. It tasted atrocious.

On another occasion, while Mom went elsewhere for some reason, he had to keep an eye on us. We had the stomach flu on this evening as well. Dad decided the cans of Campbell's chicken noodle soup selected for dinner, no doubt Mom's efforts to avoid another batch of peanut butter gravy, needed help. He sliced and fried a hefty pile of celery and added it to the soup pot. I am amazed we survived his attempts at feeding us. It took years before I could eat celery again, cooked or raw.

He did, however, make a pot of cooked dried beans with ham hocks and onion every once in awhile. He placed the washed, dried beans in an electric bean pot, the forerunner of the modern slow cooker, and then covered them with boiling water. Into the pot went the one or two ham hocks and at least one large onion, chopped. The pot cooked slowly for several hours. Before it came to the table, Dad spiced the beans with pepper, and maybe a bit more salt. That's it. Dad's method for cooking dried beans became one of my favorite foods during childhood. Cooked dried beans, whether plain like Dad's or dressed up with sauces, are a cheap and nutritious food.

There are two things to remember when cooking with dried beans.

1) The older the beans, the less moisture they contain. The dryer they are, the harder it is for them to absorb water, cook right and be edible. What is the best way to deal with those old, too-dry beans squatting in your cupboard? Recycle them: Make beanbags or heave them on the garden compost pile.

2) Never try to cook hard dried beans with acidic foods like tomatoes, or with sugar. Partially re-hydrate the beans first. Soak beans in room-temperature water for several hours or by cooking them in gently boiling water until they are mostly soft. Rehydrating beans are water-sucking little camels so make sure they are always submerged in water during the soaking/simmering process. Dried beans will expand to at least double their original size so make sure the pot is large enough. When the beans are at a good stage of softness, they break apart easily but are not mush, drain off the water, place them in the cooking pot and add the other ingredients, including those with high acid or sugar content, e.g., tomatoes, tomato sauce, BBQ sauce or pineapple, etc.

If using the amount of dried beans called for in the fol-lowing recipe, select a recently harvested variety if pos-sible. If dried beans are stored in a tight-lidded container and placed in cool, dry, dark place they will stay reason-ably hydrated for a couple of years.

I developed the recipe for **Light-in-the-Saddle Baked Beans** from one I found in a charity cookbook years ago. I rarely make it the same way twice because it is a recipe with some flexibility.

I keep all the ingredients for a pleasing pot of beans on the kitchen shelf. If we have visitors, I am prepared. After the meal and the visiting, I take satisfaction knowing my guests leave not only happy but also full of beans.

* Is someone at your table on a low-sodium diet? Substitute all the commercially canned beans listed in this recipe with rehydrated dried beans, or if available, commercially canned low-sodium beans. Be prepared to use as much as 12 cups of softened beans, maybe more. Use fried ground hamburger instead of bacon or sausage. Adjust the flavor by adding more low-sodium catsup, brown sugar or molasses and pepper. Garlic may improve the flavor of your new version of baked beans. Everyone else can add salt to his or her bowl of beans as needed. It will take time to perfect a decent, low-sodium pot of baked beans but when you do, it is worth the time involved.

LIGHT-IN-THE-SADDLE BAKED BEANS RECIPE

Ingredients:

2 28-ounce cans Bush's Baked Beans
3 15-ounce cans pork and beans
2-3 C. softened dried beans such as pinto or red,
or 3 15-ounce cans red beans
1 20-ounce can pineapple chunks, drained
1/2 C. prepared catsup
1/2 C. brown sugar
1 T. vinegar
2 T. prepared mustard
1 medium onion, chopped
1/2-1 pound precooked hamburger, sausage, bacon
or hot dogs, sliced

Directions:

Combine all ingredients, except the meat, into a large mixing bowl. Stir well. Taste and see if you need a bit more brown sugar, catsup and so forth. Add the cooked meat. Give the bean mix a good stir and pour it into two greased 9x13 pans or a greased 6-quart slow cooker. If using a slow cooker and not all the ingredients fit into it, pour the extra into a greased casserole dish or other suitable baking container, cover tightly and freeze for baking at a later time.

If you use baking pans, bake the beans uncovered at 325 degrees until the mixture bubbles in the center of each pan and some of the liquid has evaporated. Slow is the way to go when baking a pan of beans. Add a bit of water, as needed, to the beans and stir well.

If you do use a slow cooker, cook the beans on low for **at least** four hours or until the mixture is gently bubbling and the onions are soft.

Serve the Light-in-the-Saddle Baked Beans hot. A batch of beans can be chilled and served cold too.

This recipe, whether baked or unbaked, freezes well. Refrigerate all leftovers.

Cowboy Coffee

Cowboy coffee, simple to make, also goes by the name of boiled coffee or campfire coffee. Simmered long enough, it then goes by a number of picturesque names like rotgut, crankcase oil and so forth.

To make cowboy coffee requires three things: A lidded pot or kettle, coffee grounds and water. Some people would include an eggshell or two, but more about that later. Cowboy coffee is either perked or boiled until it is strong enough to drink.

I make a version of cowboy coffee in Fallon, but it is done in an old-fashioned non-electric aluminum coffee pot, like the kind used over an open campfire but on the small burner of our electric range.

My little pot consists of five pieces: the pot and its lid, the metal straw or tube, and the basket with its lid. With this simple design, the source of heat warms the water inside the pot. Once it comes to a boil, the heated water creates a type of circular displacement within the pot. During the percolation process, the boiling water in the pot goes up the tube and lands on top of the lid of the basket. Holes in this lid allow the boiling water to leak down to the coffee grounds inside the basket. The piping hot water leaches the oil and flavor out of the grounds as the tiny holes in the bottom of the basket allow the perked coffee to drip back into the water in the pot. The longer a person boils the pot, the stronger the coffee.

Here are the simple directions to make an easy and good cup of coffee when you are camping or picnicking, using the type of pot described.

Fill the pot with the desired amount of water. If you are away from a safe source of drinking water, use bottled or filtered water. Do not use any from a creek, pond or river. Even though the water in the pot comes to a rolling boil, this may not be adequate to kill any lurking parasites or harmful bacteria. (*) Don't take chances. Add the eggshells at this point. People swear it removes the excess oils from the coffee beans. I have tried it. Maybe it does, maybe it doesn't.

Place the coffee grounds inside the basket and add its flat lid. Thread the tube up through the hole in the basket. Set the lidded basket and the tube, with pedestal bottom, inside the pot filled with cold water. Add the metal lid of the coffee pot. Put the coffee pot on the heat source and bring the water in the pot to a gentle boil.

---

* If the coffee comes to a rolling boil for at least one full minute, then cools for at least 15 minutes, intestinal parasites like *Giardia* are supposed to kick the bucket. I have endured two bouts of this nasty bug, so I would definitely use bottled water, or boil the water for at least 15 minutes, let it cool, and then use the sterilized water for making coffee.

This oldie-but-goody percolation-style pot is a simple yet ingeniously designed invention.

I am afraid the modern coffee addict, those folks used to French-pressed (how that actually works is beyond me) or other snazzle-dazzle ways to make brew, would not consume this type of coffee. Most likely they would not recognize the old-fashioned stovetop type of coffee pot either, or how to put it to use. Sad.

If you cannot handle regular spine-stiffening cowboy or campfire coffee straight, then make what I call the squatte latte. Just add milk or rich cream to your boiling hot cup of perked or boiled coffee. The milk cools everything down a bit. Once the coffee is drinkable, you can squat down next to the campfire, fireplace or whatever and drink it in comfort.

Either squatte or straight, perked or boiled, whip-snap fresh coffee is a distinct pleasure, one that cannot be matched by any citified coffee shop anytime or anywhere. With steaming cup in one hand, all you need in the other grub hook is a thick, moist slice of apple kuchen or Mom's cinnamon/sugar coffee cake. The following recipe is for REAL campfire coffee, made without benefit of a coffee pot.

BOILED COWBOY COFFEE RECIPE
Ingredients and equipment:

4-5 quart kettle
Water to fill kettle, two inches from the top
1 1/2C. regular grind coffee (see directions below)

Directions:
Fill the kettle with water and bring it to a boil. Add the coffee grounds. Cover kettle with a lid if you like. Gently boil water and grinds until it is the desired strength. Shut off the burner, or remove the kettle from the campfire. Let it sit for a bit. Add a small amount of cold water, about 1/4th cup. Continue to let it sit, so the coffee grounds settle to the bottom of the kettle. Gently ladle hot coffee into mugs, or pour it into preheated insolated pot.

Recipe adapted from Cousin Shirley

What's Kuchen?

Kuchen is the German name for cake. I pronounce it "COO-kin" but my Montana relatives say, "COO-ha." Traditionally, this pastry recipe consists of a base layer of raw, sweetened yeast dough. The second layer is eggs beaten with heavy cream. Dried or fresh fruit, usually cut into slices, covers the egg mixture. A light dusting of sugar and cinnamon tops the fruit. Kuchen is divine to eat while still warm, especially when accompanied by a steaming cup of fresh-perked coffee.

Berta Lassle made the best kuchen I ever tasted, hands down. Berta, along with her young son, Helmut, came to the United States in the early 1950s as a refugee from Germany. Her first husband died during WWII. The young mother married Mom's first cousin, Christ Lassle, and settled down in Fallon to make a new life for herself and her son.

During our first days as homeowners in Fallon, Berta stopped by to introduce herself. Wayne described the initial meeting the best.

"She walked down the road from her house, introduced herself, and then decided to claim you as one of her relatives, even though you were the daughter of her deceased husband's first cousin."

Each time I saw her, we would agree to meet, someday, for coffee. But it never happened until Berta, in her blunt way, told me we better get together as she was getting old and "next time" might not happen. We set the date of our visit for next May.

When we arrived at her tiny home, the elderly but energetic woman had baked five pans of raspberry kuchen. Her cakes, a trinity of light, golden yeast bread, rich, thick, sweet custard and lightly sugared raspberries, tasted incredible. The three of us, Berta, Wayne and I, ate our way through three of them, and consumed many cups of hot coffee as we visited for the next few hours.

Berta told us of the time during WWII when she had to dig rotten potatoes from a frozen field to keep from starving, and how she, along with her infant son, hid in a ditch as planes strafed a field. During this terrible period, others told her to abandon her small son. He was a hindrance, they told her. Let him die. Nearly 60 years later, Berta's voice still held fury at the idea of abandoning her son to a certain death. She did not do the horrible thing, and that son survived, grew up in Montana and had a family of his own.

After Berta's stories ended, and as the three of us started on kuchen #4, we decided it was time to exercise some self-control, but only after downing a few pieces of it first, finishing with more cups of hot coffee. During our visit that day, and at my insistence, Berta recited to me her recipe for raspberry kuchen, as she had never written it down.

True to her prediction, Berta passed away a few months after our wonderful time together.

BERTA'S RASPBERRY KUCHEN RECIPE

Ingredients for topping:

3-6 C. fresh raspberries (or other berries or fruit)
1 stick butter
1-2 C. all-purpose flour

Directions for topping:

Wash berries and drain well. Set aside. Combine butter and flour, just enough flour to make a crumbly mixture. Set aside.

Ingredients for filling:

1C. heavy whipping cream
3 eggs
3/C. sugar
1-2 t. vanilla
2-3 T. flour (optional)

Directions for filling:

Combine ingredients and mix well. Refrigerate until ready to use.

Ingredients for dough:

6 1/2C. flour (approximate; you do not want the dough too stiff)
3/4 C. sugar
3/4 C. melted butter
3 eggs
2 packages yeast
2 C. lukewarm water

Directions for dough:

Combine 1 cup of the water and the yeast in a large bowl. Set it aside.

Stir together the eggs, 1 cup of warm water, sugar and butter. Add yeast mixture. Mix well (may use an electric mixer, but Berta probably mixed ingredients with a large spoon). Start adding the flour, 2 to 3 cups. When the beaters on the mixer cannot do their job, switch to working in the flour by hand. Knead like bread dough. Do not add too much flour or the dough will be dry. Set aside until it is raised, double in bulk. Punch down. Shape the dough into 8 or 9 balls. For each ball, roll out to size of its baking pan, plus 1 inch wider all around. Cake or pie pans work well, 8 or 9 inches in diameter. Lay yeast dough in pan. Pat it in the pan, edging up the sides of pan, about 1/2 inch or so.

To combine:

Prick dough all over with a fork. Pour the milk and egg mixture over the dough in each pan, 1/4 to 1/2 inch deep. Gently scatter fruit (the amount you wish) over top. Sprinkle crumb mixture over all this. You may also sprinkle a bit of granulated sugar and cinnamon over top of each kuchen.

Bake at 350 degrees until dough is light brown and topping gently bubbles. Makes 8-9 pans of kuchen. Refrigerate the leftovers. These baked coffee cakes freeze well.

It Might Not Be Kuchen, But ...

Mom did not prepare kuchen during our childhood. She made a variation of the German pastry, but she called it Cinnamon Coffee Cake. In my mother's kitchen coffee never accompanied this simple but heavenly-tasting treat.

For the base of the cake, Mom beat together a cake-like batter. She covered the batter with chopped walnuts harvested from our three walnut trees and granulated sugar laced with almond flavoring and cinnamon. Frugal times may have required her to skip the layer of cream and eggs, but when she made coffee cake, which was not often, we gobbled it down. Others liked it too.

The hot summer of 1957, the city decided to pave the streets in our neighborhood in northeast Portland near Rocky Butte. Mom baked several batches of her coffee cake in our hotter-than-Hades wood cook stove. She served the spicy warm cake to the large work crew, along with ice-cold Kool-Aid. Boy, were they a happy bunch when it came time for the coffee break that morning.

Coffee cake, or kuchen, whether it consists of a base made from sweet yeast bread dough, cake batter or even baking powder biscuit dough, can serve as a simple but yummy dessert. The layer of thick cream and eggs might be left out, but there must be a topping of some sort, be it fruit, nuts, spices, sugar or frosting.

Although I faithfully follow my mother's recipe for coffee cake, it doesn't taste like hers did. Perhaps what is missing is a steamy hot day in summer, a roaring wood-burning cookstove, and some burly workmen waiting in our tree-shaded front yard with tongues hanging out in hungry anticipation.

MOM'S CINNAMON COFFEE CAKE RECIPE

Ingredients for cake batter:

1 1/4 C. cake flour (see note)
1 1/4 t. baking powder
1/4 t. salt
3 T. butter or other shortening
2/3 C. sugar
1 egg, beaten
5 T. milk

Ingredients for crumb topping:

1 1/2 T. butter
4 T. all-purpose flour
2 T. powdered sugar
Dash salt
1/4 t. cinnamon
Few drops of almond extract
1/4-1/2 C. chopped walnuts

Directions for crumb topping:

Mix together the flour, sugar, salt and cinnamon. Add butter and flavoring. With a spoon or with your hands, work together the ingredients until crumbly in texture. Add the chopped walnuts and mix well. Set aside.

Directions for batter:
Sift together the flour, baking powder and salt. Cream together the butter and sugar. Add egg and beat until ingredients are fluffy. Add flour mix and the milk, alternately, to the creamed butter, sugar and egg. Beat after each addition. Pour batter into a greased and flour-dusted 8 or 9-inch cake pan. Sprinkle the sugar/cinnamon/nut mixture over the top.

Bake at 350 degrees until a toothpick stuck in the middle comes out clean, or 30 minutes. Serve warm, but cold will also do nicely. Refrigerate leftovers.

Note: If you use all-purpose flour instead of cake flour, remember it is denser than cake flour. To remedy this, measure a full cup of sifted all-purpose flour and then remove 2 level tablespoons. For the topping, remove 1 1/2 teaspoons of flour.

Cookie Monsters

Wave a plate of warm chocolate chip-filled cookies under the nose of a hungry farmer, child, neighbor or boss and you will see a human transformed into a cookie monster.

People love to eat cookies. This is true most anywhere in the United States, and it is true for Montanans as well. These bits of baked goods, crammed with chocolate chips, coconut, peanuts, jam or other mouth-watering goodies, are not once-in-a-while treats but regular stand-bys in the daily diet. Drop or bar cookies are the easiest to prepare, bake and serve. They can be eaten out of hand while on the way to school, the barn or town. Slip a couple of moist, spicy banana bars into a brown-bag lunch and the rest of the day brightens up.

Bar cookies seem especially favored in rural areas. They are quick to make, and they freeze well. Any respectable family gathering, be it a branding, church potluck or funeral dinner, will feature at least one plate of them.

If you are not a cookie eater and don't make them for others, I suggest you change your ways. Everybody should have mastered at least one decent cookie recipe. When you do craft a good one, potlucks or other gatherings will never again be a cause for anxiety. Where to find a good cookie recipe? Do like the rest of us often do: Steal someone else's.

Check out the cookies being served at the next family gathering, funeral or staff potluck. If you find a really tasty one, hunt down the person who brought them and ask for the recipe. Do not let it end there. Not only ask for the recipe, ask the lucky one to tell you what makes his or her batch of cookies so good-tasting. Once you get your hands on the recipe, make a batch. Don't get discouraged if the first try doesn't quite measure up. Don't give up.

Ask the giver of the recipe for specifics. Did he use the shortening called for, or butter instead? Was it cream instead of milk? Did he sneak in one more egg than the recipe stated? Once you have the cookie recipe under control, tweak the ingredients to make it yours. For example, if the recipe calls for raisins but raisins remind you of dead flies or the kids won't eat them, try substituting chocolate chips.

I have included only two recipes for cookies, and they are good ones. The banana bars are even better after they have been baked, frozen and then frosted as the batch thaws. When Shirley's recipe, which I call **Marshmallow Peanut Butter Bars,** shows up at a gathering, it is fun to watch well-behaved adults turn into craven cookie monsters – the cookies are that good to eat.

People love to eat cookies, so spiff up your ability to make a tastebud-tingling, lip-sucking batch of them. Make it your time to go out there and tame the cookie monsters lurking at your house, where you work, or even sitting next to you in the pew each Sunday.

BUST-THEM-UP BANANA BARS RECIPE

Ingredients:

1/2 C. butter
1 1/2 C. granulated sugar
2 eggs
3/4 C. buttermilk
1 t. baking soda
3 ripe bananas, mashed
1/2 t. salt
1/2 t. vanilla
2 C. all-purpose flour
3/4 C. chopped nuts

Directions:

Cream together the butter and sugar until both are light and fluffy. Add the eggs and beat until the batter is smooth and all the ingredients are well incorporated. Combine the buttermilk with the bananas; beat ingredients again, and then set aside the bowl.

Sift together the dry ingredients. Combine, on an alternating basis, the buttermilk and bananas, then the dry ingredients. Mix only until everything is well blended. Don't overbeat the batter.

Pour the batter into a greased and floured 10x15 jelly roll pan. A 9x13-inch works too. Bake at 350 degrees until it passes the toothpick test. Dust with powdered sugar, or cool the cake and then spread it with the following recipe:

Frosting:

1 1/2 C. sifted powdered sugar
6 T. softened butter
6 T. milk or cream
1/2 t. vanilla
Add all ingredients in a quart-sized bowl. Beat until creamy and smooth. Spread on cooled cake.

Note: I credited this recipe to Aunt Pauline Gaub, as I have a copy in her handwriting, but Shirley says it is her Aunt Linda Irion's recipe. Linda is Pauline's baby sister. I love Banana Bars regardless of which recipe was whose.

MARSHMALLOW PEANUT BUTTER BARS RECIPE

Ingredients:

1 box yellow cake mix

2/3 C. margarine or butter

1 egg

3 1/2 C. miniature marshmallows

2/3 C. corn syrup

2 T. vanilla

1/4 C. margarine or butter

1 1/2 C. peanut butter chips

2 C. salted peanuts

Directions:

Combine the cake mix, margarine or butter, and egg together in a small bowl. Transfer the dough to a lightly greased 10x15 inch pan. Pat the dough down. Bake for 10-15 minutes at 325 degrees. Remove pan and top the batter with the marshmallows. Bake an additional 7-10 minutes. Cool.

Heat the syrup, vanilla, 1/4 C. margarine and peanut butter chips in a pan, until chips are melted. Pour over the cooled marshmallows. Top with salted peanuts. Press the peanuts into the syrup and vanilla mix. Cover and refrigerate. To serve, cut into bars. For a thicker cookie, use a 9x13 pan.

Recipe by La Vonne Sackman. From: "Community Presbyterian Church Cookbook". Terry, Montana.

We'll-Fool-'Em Cake and Frostings

When invited to dinner or some other event requiring donations of food, a think-ahead gal or gent comes bearing gifts, not empty-handed and hoping for a mooch. Arrive with a lip-smacking, naughty-rich chocolate **Crazy Day Chocolate Cake** in hand and you will score points with someone, for sure, and keep your caboose out of a tight corner to boot.

I've made this recipe for cake for more than 40 years. Someone gave it to me while we lived on Kosrae, a small island in Micronesia. Just about every church or charity cookbook contains a variation of this recipe. There are six reasons it is worth your time to try the recipe:

- It defies the rules of traditional cake making.
- The recipe is easy to prepare.
- It requires few ingredients, a bonus if staples are limited or it's just one of those crazy days.
- The recipe is almost mistake-proof.
- You end up with a moist, dense chocolate cake.

I have included two recipes for frosting: chocolate mocha and German chocolate. Each one gives this plain cake a different presentation.

For a more moist cake, after the cake has cooled, wrap it in tin foil and freeze it for at least eight hours. Remove the cake from the freezer at least three hours before the event. Frost while it is still frozen. If you have a two-layer cake, frost each layer and set them on the serving dish. Cover the cake and allow it to defrost at room temperature and then watch your dessert take the cake over all the others.

CRAZY DAY CHOCOLATE CAKE RECIPE
Ingredients:

3 C. sifted all-purpose flour
6 T. baking cocoa powder
2 t. soda
2 C. granulated sugar
1 t. salt
2/3 C. oil
2 T. vinegar
2 t. vanilla
2 C. water

Directions:
Sift the first five ingredients into a large mixing bowl. Burrow three holes into the dry ingredients. In the first hole, pour the oil. Pour the vinegar in the second hole. The third hole gets the vanilla. Pour the two cups of water over the other ingredients in the bowl. Vigorously hand-beat the mixture for 60 strokes. Blend the ingredients well, but do not whup the daylights out of the batter. Only 60 strokes!

Pour the batter into a greased and floured 9x13 pan, or two 9-inch cake pans. If using two cake pans, grease the bottoms of both pans, cover each bottom with waxed paper cut to size, then grease and flour the wax paper. Bake at 350 degrees for 30 minutes or until a toothpick, inserted into the middle of each pan, comes out clean.

Allow the cake to cool for five minutes. If you used two round cake pans, carefully run a dinner knife around the outer edge of the baked cakes. Place a cooling rack, or a dinner plate over the top of one of the layers. Quickly flip both the cake and the plate/rack over. Once the cake is completely out of the pan, flip it right-side-up onto a cooling rack or dinner plate lined with wax paper. Do the same with the second layer of baked cake.

Whether it's baked in a 9x13 pan, two layer pans or cupcake molds, allow the cake to thoroughly cool before frosting. As mentioned earlier, I often wrap each cooled layer in tinfoil and freeze it. I also freeze the 9x13-sized cake, still in the pan, overnight and then frost it before it thaws. This cake moistens with time. Keep refrigerated.

CHOCOLATE MOCHA-MINT FROSTING RECIPE
Ingredients:

5-6 C. powdered sugar, sifted and then measured
1/4 C. powdered baking cocoa
1/4-1/2 C. butter, softened
1 t. vanilla flavoring
1 t. peppermint flavoring
1/4 C. strong coffee, either brewed or instant
Pinch of salt
Chopped walnuts, grated semi-sweet chocolate or crushed peppermint candies

Directions:

Sift together the powdered sugar and the cocoa. Add the butter and beat until all of it is well blended. Add the flavorings, hot coffee and a pinch of salt. Beat the frosting until creamy smooth. Frost the cake. If you like, garnish top of cake with chopped walnuts, grated semi-sweet chocolate or crushed candies. The amount of frosting in this recipe will cover a two-layer cake, a 9x13 pan or 1-2 dozen cupcakes.

Note: I do not know the origins of this recipe but a former neighbor in Crabtree, Jan White, shared her version of it nearly 40 years ago. Thanks, Jan. As usual, I fiddled with it a bit.

COCONUT-NUT FROSTING RECIPE
Ingredients:

12 T. unsalted butter, (1 1/2 sticks)
1 C. packed brown sugar
1/2 C. light cream
2 C. shredded coconut
1 C. chopped walnuts or pecans
2 eggs, well beaten
1 t. vanilla

Directions:
Combine the butter, brown sugar, cream, eggs and vanilla in a heavy 2-quart saucepan. Stir until all the ingredients are thoroughly blended. Heat the mixture, starting temperature out on medium or medium-low heat. Stir often. Raise the temperature a bit if needed, but not too high. Cook until mixture thickens, about 10 minutes. Add both the coconut and the chopped nuts.

Beat the mixture with a rubber spatula or wooden spoon until thick enough to spread. If you made two layers of **Crazy Day Chocolate Cake**, spread part the frosting over the top of the *lower* layer of cake first. Be generous. Place the second layer on top of the first. Frost only the top of the second layer and let it drizzle down the sides of the cake. The coconut-nut frosting mixture thickens as it cools. If you make a sheet cake, spread the entire top of the cake with the frosting.

Serve plain or with vanilla ice cream.

Note: Oregonian Jean McAtee gave me this frosting recipe the first year or so of my marriage. I love it. Thank you, Jean, and enjoy finishing your eighth decade of living.

Note: When you use this recipe for frosting on the **Crazy Day Chocolate Cake**, people might be fooled into thinking it is an authentic German chocolate cake, which it is not. The ingredients for a German chocolate cake batter are different, but so what? People will gobble down your version nonetheless.

Dumplings, Knipfla and Noodles

Dumplings, knipfla* (pronounced "NIP-flah") and noodles are three culinary sisters. These simple recipes share the basic ingredients of flour, liquid, leavening agent and salt. Eggs are often added to increase the richness of the dough and to serve as a binding agent. All three wheat-flour-based products must be cooked with liquid. Each is gently boiled in water or broth or placed on top of stewing meat and steamed until done.

Just about every cultural group represented in the United States has its version of German knipfla, basic dumplings or noodles. The cook in the family might make them on a regular basis, and they often serve as comfort food to the family. These dishes are inexpensive staples in the diet and fill a person up.

Mom made flour dumplings throughout my early childhood. She might prepare a batch around the time I arrived home from school, or as I came in from playing

---

* Knipfla, like many other recipes handed down by Germans-from-Russia immigrants, is spelled phonetically. Some other titles for the same (or similar) recipe: knefflin, knoepfla and nefla.

outside on a chilly afternoon in autumn or winter. While chatting with me, she plopped spoonfuls of raw dough on top of a cut-up, boiled stewing hen hunkered down in a large cooking pot. Mom made sure the bird rubbed wings with simmering onions, carrots and celery. As she put the lid on the pot, I received the usual admonishment.

"Don't go too far away because dinner will be ready in about 20 minutes." With inviting aromas like that, I stayed close at hand.

I make dumplings every now and then. The recipe is not hard to master. Just be sure the dough contains enough flour to make it stiff and that each dumpling rides atop the braising pot roast, chicken or other meat. Small bits of dumpling dough also work well in soups such as chicken, red meat or vegetable.

Knipfla came into the extended Gaub family through my Uncle Henry's wife, Pauline. To me, the food seems like a cross between a small dumpling and a thick noodle.

The bare-bones recipe requires few ingredients: flour, water or other liquid, and salt. If the cook adds baking powder and beaten eggs, the dough is more flavorful, holds together better, and expands during the cooking process. I recommend the enriched recipe.

Traditional knipfla, Kalmback-style, is often served with boiled potatoes and topped with bread cubes or crumbs sautéed in oil or butter. I like knipfla simmered in beef or chicken broth and presented as a side dish. The first time I tasted it, I was hooked. Knipfla does take time to make but is well worth the effort.

Noodle dough, like knipfla, is worked with a rolling pin or by hand. A recipe for plain noodles shares most of the ingredients with its two sisters, but the dough is rolled flatter than a pancake, cut into strips and steamed or boiled. I have made homemade noodles a time or two through the years, but knipfla and dumplings take far less time and fuss.

If you want to try making wheat noodles, be prepared to spend hours at it and possibly make a horrendous mess in the kitchen. They can be fun to make, especially if you take on the adventure with children or other family members. I do not include a recipe for homemade noodles, but one can be found in an all-purpose cookbook or on the Internet.

As busy as you might be, do not dismiss the idea of learning to make steamed dumplings, knipfla or noodles. It may be just the thing to brighten up a cold, dreary winter day. Allow plenty of time and use a covered tabletop, large cutting board or a generous amount of counter space. Who knows? You might discover the family not only likes to eat one of these simple recipes, it also becomes a part of your family's culinary history.

EASY-DO DUMPLINGS RECIPE
Ingredients:

2 C. all-purpose flour, more as needed

1 T. plus 1 t. baking powder

1/4 t. salt

3/4 C. water or cold chicken, pork, beef or vegetable broth

1/4 C. olive or salad oil

Directions:

Sift together the dry ingredients. Do not skip this step as the baking powder must be well incorporated throughout the other dry ingredients. Combine broth and oil. Add to dry ingredients and stir them together until barely moist. Sprinkle a bit of flour over dough and turn one or two times with a rubber spatula. Sprinkle more flour over exposed wet area and turn. You want a stiff dough but not too dry. Add more flour if needed. Do not overwork the dough.

With the spatula, scoop out pieces of raw dough, each one the size of a large plum, until all the dough is shaped. Place them on a floured plate or cutting board. Remove the lid from a wide-bottomed pot of simmering pot roast, chicken or vegetables. Place the dumplings **on top** of the meat, etc., with the broth or juice barely touching the bottom of the raw dumplings, if at all. Leave a bit of room between each one. Cover the pot with a tight-fitting lid and bring to a gentle boil. Allow the dumplings to steam for 15-20 minutes or until the interior of one looks cooked. Makes 8 to 10 dumplings. Refrigerate leftovers.

Note: If you want a more nutritious dumpling, use milk in place of the water or broth.

AUNT PAULINE'S KNIPFLA RECIPE
Ingredients:

3-4 C. all-purpose flour
3/4-1 C. cold water
1 1/2t. salt
1 egg
3/4 t. baking powder
Water or broth

Directions:

Combine the water and egg; mix well. Set aside. Sift together 3 cups of the flour, salt and baking powder. Add the liquid to the dry ingredients, a bit at a time, enough to make a stiff dough. Adjust the consistency of the dough with a bit more liquid or flour if needed.

By hand or with a rolling pin, pat or roll the dough to about 1 1/2 inches thick. Be sure to keep both the dough and the cutting surface well floured. For easier handling, cut the dough into long strips two to three inches wide.

With a knife or food scissors, snip off several pieces from the strips or the flat and rectangular shaped dough, each about the size of a nickel. Place these pieces on a well-floured surface. Dust with flour. Continue until all the dough is cut up.

Bring the water or broth to a gentle boil. Add knipfla a few pieces at a time until all are in the pot. Cover pot and simmer until tender. Remove knipfla to a large bowl and toss with butter, salt and pepper. Serve it with the broth if you like.

Note: Aunt Pauline, and her daughter, Shirley, often prepared a large frying pan of peeled, cubed potatoes, each cube 1-2 inches in size. The potatoes were boiled gently in salted water or chicken broth while the women cut up the knipfla dough into pieces. A person could also use a Dutch oven or other larger, lidded kettle or pot. They placed the bits of raw knipfla dough atop the spuds and added more liquid, enough to barely cover them but not the knipfla. The pot was covered and allowed to gently simmer until the knipfla steamed. They removed the finished potatoes along with the cooked knipfla and placed both in a large serving bowl. After carefully stirring the two together, until the potatoes broke apart, they might add generous dots of butter and dashes of salt and pepper to taste.

German Rice Rolls

My maternal grandmother, Christina Hettich Gaub, made German rice/cabbage rolls, and it is one of the few authentic German recipes to trickle down our family tree. Since living part-time in Montana, I have discovered each maternal aunt had her variation of this dish, and Mom's version was particularly wonderful.

Before my marriage to Wayne, she made a big batch and served them to us. At the mention of rice, my fiancé started to whine, but once his large Swedish nose sniffed the spicy sausage, once he inhaled the mingled fragrances of beef, tomato, cabbage and sage, Wayne zipped his lips. After Mom presented the main dish, he opened those lips, cheerfully working his way through several plump, meaty servings. If a future mother-in-law could cook like that, perhaps his mind reasoned, this was one man who would not go hungry.

When my husband and our three children traveled to Germany the summer of 1985, we stumbled onto the Bessarabian-German Museum in Stuttgart. This museum honored those Germans who immigrated to

Bessarabia, the name for an area located within a massive, funnel shaped portion of land in old Russia, north of the Black Sea.

The museum in Stuttgart fascinated me. Though my grandparents were not Bessarabian Germans, Grandmother Gaub's fine crocheting and embroidery were similar to the displays in the museum. German-Bessarabian clothing and accessories look much like what my grandparents and others ancestors wore during that time period. Two of Mom's sisters, Martha and Emma, told me Grandfather tanned hides and worked with leather, and also did wrought-iron work. I saw evidence of those skills in the little museum as well.

After our tour, the curator asked our family, "Would you like to eat an authentic German-Bessarabian meal?" Of course we would! Before long, he ushered us downstairs to the tiny restaurant in the lower level of the museum.

The main dish was no stranger to my family: German rice rolls. As much as I savored this meal, served to us in its unique location, the dish did not surpass my mother's variation. Nonetheless, now when I make rice rolls I am transported back to that museum, back to that astounding day, and even further back to the dinner table of my childhood.

Mom never used a written recipe for her version of rice rolls. With my prodding, she wrote it down late in her life. Sadly, no matter how I try, I do not make them as rich and flavorful as she could. I passed on her recipe, with detailed explanation, to each of my children. They are the fourth generation, at least, to make rice rolls. One of the times my grandchildren visit us, I hope to introduce them to this piece of our family history.

GRANDMA ANNA'S GERMAN RICE ROLLS RECIPE

Ingredients:

One large head of cabbage, core removed
3/4 C. uncooked rice
1 1/2 C. water
1/2 pound pork sausage or unseasoned ground pork
1 pound hamburger
1 medium onion, chopped fine
2 cloves of garlic, finely minced (optional)
1/8 t. ground pepper
1 t. salt
1/2-1 t. ground sage or poultry seasoning
3 C. canned stewed tomatoes
1/4-1/3 C. brown sugar

Directions:

Pour 2-3 inches of water into a large kettle. Bring to a boil. Place the head of cabbage in kettle, cored side down, and steam until its outer leaves wilt. Do not allow water to stay at a rapid boil or the cabbage will overcook, with the leaves turning mushy. Remove cabbage from kettle and let it cool and drain. Peel off all the limp outer leaves. As you work to its core, if you have larger leaves that are not limp, they can still be used for wrapping the meat mix. Aunt Emma told me she always cut out the tough, thick center spine from each of the largest cabbage leaves. This gives two good-sized leaves from the one. Slice into wedges the uncooked core section of the head of cabbage. Set them aside.

Bring 1 1/2 cups of water to a boil. Add rice, cover with lid and turn down heat to low. Cook rice for 5-8 minutes. The rice should be partially cooked. Remove from heat, drain off excess liquid, and cool rice in a separate bowl.

Combine the ground meats, cooled rice, chopped onion, garlic and seasonings in a large bowl. If you used unseasoned ground pork, be prepared to add a bit more seasonings. Mix well with your hands.

Put a small handful of meat/rice mixture in the center of a cabbage leaf. Fold outer edges of leaf around the meat, like an envelope. Place the roll, flaps side down, in a sturdy cooking kettle with lid. Let each roll snuggle up to the next one. Stagger the layers. This allows the steam from the water to move evenly throughout the kettle of cooking rolls.

Top the rolls with leftover wedges of cabbage. Pour the canned tomatoes over all. Sprinkle the brown sugar over the top of rolls. Add extra ground pepper if you like. Cover and bring kettle to a boil. Turn down the heat. The liquid in the kettle should remain at a gentle boil, being careful to not burn the bottom layer of the rolls. Boil 1 1/2to 2 hours or until they are well cooked. Serve piping hot. Mom always served the cabbage rolls with fluffy mashed potatoes. The broth from the cooked rolls can be used as light sauce or gravy for the mashed potatoes. Chill leftovers in a shallow pan. Cooked German rice rolls taste even better the second day. They freeze well too.

Pumpkin Blossoms

Pumpkin blossoms are a simple pastry often eaten out of hand. My mother's recipe called for cooked spiced pumpkin enclosed in a crust of pastry dough and then baked in the oven. Although she called them pumpkin blossoms, other similar recipes found in old German/Eastern European community cookbooks published in the U.S. are titled blachinda, plachinta, kerbin burock and pumpkin tarts.

The name of this Germans-from-Russia recipe probably comes from both its filling and its shape. A spoonful of the spiced pumpkin is placed in the center of a circle of pastry dough. The opposite outer edges of the dough are folded together two by two and then pinched together so it looks like the open bloom of a flower. During the baking process, the filling oozes out of the pinched-together edges, thereby creating the center of the bloom.

I ate both pumpkin and apple blossoms throughout childhood but have seldom made them for my family. Our kids ate them at Grandma's, however, and never forgot the experience.

"I plan to include a few of Grandma Anna's recipes in the book," I told our daughter Sharon during one of her recent visits to Montana from Alaska.

"Which ones are you planning to use?" she asked.

"There will be rice rolls," I replied.

"Don't forget Grandma's pumpkin blossoms," she added. Aha! Sharon remembered the baked pastry after all these years. I included her request.

Other cultures have their version of this simple pastry/main dish.

A few years back, I ate the Romanian variation, called plachinda/plachinta. This cook's recipe called for unsweetened yeast bread dough. She divided the dough into globs the size of baseballs, rolled each one out to about one inch thick, and then placed a large spoonful of fine shredded raw cabbage in the center of each circle of the flattened dough. A Romanian cook might use whatever was on hand: shredded vegetables, apples or other fruit, minced meat or spices. The woman gathered the outer edges of the dough together and pinched it into a closed pouch. After dusting the pouch with flour, she turned it upside down.

After it had set for a while, she rolled each pouch to about one-half inch thick using a wooden dowel. The filling became incorporated throughout the dough during the rolling-out process. The cook fried each flattened

pouch in hot oil, one or two at a time. Romanian pla-
chinda is served piping hot, room temperature, or even
chilled.

Pumpkin blossoms are a treat to eat. When I do make
them for our grandchildren they will become at least the
fifth generation to experience this simple, spicy pastry.

PUMPKIN BLOSSOMS RECIPE
Ingredients:

2 C. cooked and mashed pumpkin (commercially canned pumpkin works well)
1/4 -1/2 C. sugar
1/4 -1/ 2 t. cinnamon
Water
Pastry dough (use recipe found in this section)
Small dots or pats of butter

Directions:
Make a batch of **Roll Over Easy Pastry Crust**, the last recipe listed in this section of the book. Pull off parts of the dough and form each one into a ball the size of a small apple. Roll each one to about 1/4 inch thick. Let circles of dough rest a few minutes.

Place mashed pumpkin in a bowl. Add the sugar and cinnamon. Cream the ingredients together with an electric mixture. If the pumpkin seems too thick to beat, add a bit of water. The filling should not be thin and runny. Add more cinnamon and sugar to taste if needed.

With a dinner spoon, put a generous dollop of pumpkin mix in the center of each circle. Add a pat of butter. Mentally divide the circle into six sections. Bring together the outer edges of the dough, two opposite sections at a time. Think of the two edges as opposite positions on a clock, i.e. 12 o'clock and 6 o'clock, 2 o'clock and 8 o'clock, 3 o'clock and 9 o'clock.

Lift the opposite edges of the pastry dough, and pinch them together for an inch or two. Do the same with the other sections of the dough, pinching them together with first two sections, and so on. The goal is to have the outer edges of the pastry pinched together so the all filling will not ooze out. If possible, gently shape the folded edge of the dough so it resembles the petals of a flower. Sprinkle the top with more cinnamon and sugar.

With a metal spatula, place blossoms on a lightly greased cookie sheet. Bake at 350 degrees until the crust is light-golden brown. Serve warm or cold. Refrigerate leftovers.

Note: Mom often used sliced apples instead of pumpkin. When she did, we called them apple blossoms.

Custard's Last Stand

Mom pulled open the oven door of the fired-up wood cook stove. The melded fragrances of vanilla and cinnamon floated out. Before long, those tantalizing aromas drifted forth from her version of Aladdin's Cave and into the rest of the house. Once my kid nose took notice, I had to find the source of olfactory pleasure. It was not hard to do. I just followed the pull of the luxurious perfume of vanilla and cinnamon.

Would it be rich rice custard? Or maybe it would be bread pudding, loaded with raisins, fresh milk and eggs. Either way, it meant treat time tonight.

"You cannot eat the dessert now or it will spoil your dinner," Mom said after one look at me. This goody was worth the wait. Old-fashioned rice custard and bread pudding were two soul foods of my childhood.

What is custard? How does a person define a pudding?

Plain custard consists of eggs, milk or cream, sugar, flavoring and maybe a spice or two. Soft custard is cooked on top the stove using a double boiler. For firm custard, the cook combines the ingredients and pours them into custard cups or a larger baking dish. Those baking cups or dish are placed in a pan of water and baked in a 350-degree oven until a knife stuck in the middle of the cup comes out clean. With both methods, the eggs thicken and solidify the milk as they cook.

A pudding, on the other hand, means different things to different people. In the United Kingdom, pudding is any dessert served after the main meal. For Americans, a pudding might consist of eggs, cream or milk, sugar and vanilla, such as the custard mentioned earlier, or something quite different. Confused? Let me explain it further.

America cooks, especially in past decades, added other ingredients to the basic custard recipe of eggs, milk, sweetener, and flavoring. A wide variety of foods, such as stale bread, dried or fresh fruit, grated carrots, sweet potato or rice, were plowed in with the eggs and milk. With this variation, the milk provided protein and supplied the moisture needed to lubricate the dry ingredients. The eggs added more protein and bound the foods together. The addition of a fruit or vegetable supplied vitamins, and the bread, rice or grains gave the consumer much needed carbohydrates. Flavorings and spices added zip. Sometimes a bit of sugar sweetened the deal. Puddings were either steamed in a pan of water atop the stove or baked in the oven. A well-built pudding proved appetizing and provided energy and nutrition, and all for a small monetary outlay.

In October 2008 I attended a tasting party hosted by the Oregon State University Libraries Special Collections & Archives Research Center. In conjunction with American Archives Month, the library gathered up historical recipes, most of them developed from 1916 to 1939 by the Oregon State University Extension Service. For the October party, people from the archives research center prepared recipes from this collection. It astounded me how many of the main-dish recipes prepared, such as cheese pudding, carrot omelet and rice spoon bread, consisted of few ingredients, no meat, and were heavy on carbohydrates. Each also contained a good amount of eggs, cheese or milk and sometimes all three. During those years, people who worked long, hard days needed large amounts of carbohydrates and protein to keep going. Those simple, cheap and hearty recipes gave men, women and children the energy they needed.

Even now, feeding people rich, hearty custards and puddings for dessert or even as a main dish is one of the cook's secrets to getting by during an economic squeeze especially if eggs and milk are less expensive and/or more plentiful.

The practice of indulging in these custard-based foods nearly suffered its last stand when people moved off the farm, the family purse filled up, and it became fashionable to push for lighter eating patterns. All those eggs and cream, all that carbohydrates in one's diet became verboten. Besides, people decided making something from scratch, even simple scratch, took too much time and energy after a long day at work.

But when personal income tightens, or even slides into a bottomless sinkhole, folks' attitudes shift as well. The cook starts looking for and trying out thrifty recipes from the past. Why not? The person in charge of meals needs something simple to make that feeds the family and offers nutritive value. That individual wants something tasty, and hearty enough to keep the hungry humans under his/her care satisfied, and on the cheap. That means back to the basics. Custards and puddings stand a chance once again, often with an updated and creative twist.

Skip the cream and use skim milk. Still add those eggs, because the latest nutrition news is that those little guys are healthy to eat. All those hens knew what they were doing after all. Tone down the sugar content. Try tweaking pudding and custard recipes by adding an unusual herb like rosemary or a spice like cardamom. Sneak in some grated carrot or sweet potato. But at this point I need to add a word of caution: Use the different only if your family is familiar with it and likes what you snuck in.

Despite a need to keep one eyeball on my calories and cholesterol, I admit the truth. When I eat bread pudding filled with so many raisins they look like cows bumping into each other in a loading chute, it is time to forget the calories, forget the present. I am back at my childhood home in Portland, spooning into the long-awaited dessert. Our family of four is together once again, even if it is only for a few precious moments.

GRANDMA ANNA'S BREAD PUDDING RECIPE
Ingredients:

2 C. stale bread, cubed

3 eggs, beaten

1/3 C. granulated or brown sugar

1/4 t. ground cinnamon, plus some for dusting top of pudding

1 t. vanilla

2 C. whole milk (here's where you slip in the skim)

1/2 -1 C. dried raisins, more if you like, (may substitute dried cranberries or chopped, dried apricots)

Directions:

Beat together the eggs and milk. Add sugar, cinnamon and vanilla. Mix well. Fold in the stale breadcrumbs and dried fruit. Again, mix well, so the bread and other fillers are saturated with the liquid. Dust with more cinnamon if you like.

Pour into an 8x8-inch greased baking dish. Place the dish inside a larger baking pan. Fill the larger pan with hot water until it measures one inch up the sides of the smaller one. Place both pans in the oven.

Bake at 325 degrees, 30-45 minutes, or until a knife, stuck in the center of the pudding comes out clean and the top of the pudding is light brown. Do not bake it too long. Allow the bread pudding to set for 10-15 minutes. Serve hot. Some people pour a vanilla or hard sauce over the pudding just before eating, but my mother served it plain. Why not try low-fat yogurt as topping?

Refrigerate the leftovers.

SHIRLEY'S BAKED RICE RECIPE
Ingredients:

1 C. long-grained rice, uncooked
1 C. sugar
1 C. milk
1 C. cream
3 eggs
I t. vanilla
Cinnamon
1/2-1 C. raisins (optional)

Directions:
Cook rice according to the directions on the package. Allow rice to cool.

Mix eggs, sugar, cream and milk together in a large bowl and beat well. Fold in cooked rice (and raisins if you like) and pour into a greased 8x10-inch or 9x9-inch pan. Sprinkle top with cinnamon.

Bake at 325 degrees 30-45 minutes until firm and knife comes out of center clean. Shirley cooks her rice until the custard is **just** set. Cool slightly and serve during the main meal or as a dessert.

Refrigerate the leftovers.

Seasons of Pie

We have a small summer garden at our home in Fallon. Snuggled up to it on the west side is a long, handsome row of rhubarb. When in Montana, if a person thinks of pie, often she or he thinks of rhubarb. Connect both and you come up with a hot, tart-sweet popular dessert few Montanans reject. Rhubarb is one edible plant able to survive the deep, cold winters, burning-hot summers and hordes of devouring hoppers, all regular visitors to the eastern part of the state.

Mom enjoyed baking, and homemade pies were her specialty. During my growing-up years, Mom's pies chronicled each season of the year.

As spring eased winter out of the picture, it partnered with tart rhubarb pie. The months of June and July, we counted on fresh raspberry pie, topped with sweet, thick whipped cream. Blackberry or peach carried us through the summer months. Autumn rolled in with apple pie, thick with juicy apples covered in cinnamon-spiced syrup. Pumpkin and mincemeat announced Thanksgiving and Christmas. Winter forced us to take a break, but with the month of March, we knew it was time for rhubarb pie season all over again.

When making her pies, Mom used fresh fruit and baked each pie at low heat (300-325 degrees) until the top crust turned a beautiful golden brown. We did not suffer a runny filling, because the slow heat of our wood-fueled oven drew out the excess moisture in a way seldom achieved with gas or electric. At least that's how I explain it. No one else made a wild Himalayan blackberry pie like her. From my point of view nobody bested any of Mom's pies.

I cannot give you the recipe for my mother's piecrust, as she never used one. Her dough consisted of flour, shortening, salt and a bit of water. She knew how to handle the dough with finesse as the crusts on all of her pies turned out flaky and tender.

In the first years of my marriage, despite a college degree in home economics, I couldn't make a decent piecrust to save my hide. Fortunately, someone gave me an almost foolproof recipe. If you look through an old community or church-sponsored cookbook, a variation of it is bound to be included. This recipe defies the rules. In addition to flour, solid fat, salt and water, it calls for an egg, sugar, baking powder and vinegar. With this crust, there is less need to use a light hand while incorporating the water with the combined flour and fat. Perhaps the vinegar helps maintain the crust's flaky tenderness in some way. Never one to leave anything alone, I tried the recipe using four types of solid fats: rendered pork fat, butter, margarine and commercial shortening. I think Crisco© works the best.

This pie dough is quite tolerant. On short schedule, I have dumped all of the ingredients together in a bowl, worked it up with my hands, and still had an edible product. Most times I take care when making the recipe, but harried days sometimes call for harried measures.

For many years, throughout the late summer and early fall I made around three dozen two-crust fruit pies. I wrapped each one in tin foil, labeled the top and then froze it, unbaked, until needed. When the time came, I placed the unwrapped but still frozen pie on a cookie sheet. I covered the fluted edges of the two sealed crusts with foil and placed the pie into a preheated 300-to 350-degree oven. The pie baked until the crust turned a light golden brown and the filling bubbled out through the slits cut in the top crust.

As with most cooks and handed-down recipes, the one for piecrust found in this book is somewhat different from the original given to me more than four decades ago. At least I think it is. Maybe not. The recipe still works for me and I believe you will find it satisfactory as well. My mother ate quite a few pieces of my pies during her lifetime and never made negative comments concerning the condition of the crust, so it must have met her approval. Either that or Mom exhibited self-control, good manners and a strong stomach.

Virginia A. Johnson

RHUBARB PIE FILLING RECIPE
Ingredients:

4-6 C. fresh rhubarb, washed and cut into 1/2-inch slices
1-2 C. granulated sugar, depending on whether you like a tart pie, or sweeter
1/3 C. all-purpose flour
1/4 t. cinnamon
3 T. butter

Directions:
Combine the rhubarb, sugar, flour and cinnamon. Pour the rhubarb mix into a pastry-lined 9-inch pie plate. If there is more filling than the plate will hold, set it aside. The rhubarb mix will cook down a bit, but use your best judgment. Cut the butter into six pieces. Dot the top of the filling with them. Cover the filling with the second crust. Pinch together the outer edges of the piecrust. Cover these edges with strips of tinfoil. Cut slits in the top of the crust so steam from the hot filling will escape. Bake at 350 degrees until filling bubbles out of the steam vents, 45-60 minutes.

If you live in strawberry country, replace 1/3 to 1/2 of the rhubarb with fresh or frozen strawberries.

ROLL-OUT-EASY PASTRY CRUST RECIPE
Ingredients:

4 C. all-purpose flour
1 t. salt (I omit the salt)
1 t. baking powder (I use half this amount)
1-2 T. granulated sugar
1 1/2C. Crisco© shortening
1 egg
1 T. vinegar
1/2 C. cold water (maybe more, maybe less)

Directions:
Dough recipe:
Sift together the flour, salt and baking powder. Stir in the sugar.

Work in the shortening by hand. For half of the flour mixture, the fat globules should be the size of peas; the rest of the mixture has the texture of corn-meal. Combine the eggs, vinegar and water and beat well. Pour that mixture over the dry ingredients and gently work the dough by hand or with a fork until all the moisture is incorporated. If the dough seems a bit dry and crumbly, sprinkle on more water a tablespoon at a time. The dough must have enough liquid to bind ingredients together; otherwise the crust will crumble as it is rolled out.

Form the dough into four balls. Allow them to rest, covered, for at least 30 minutes if you have the time. I often refrigerate the dough and make the pies the next day. If you do this, allow the dough to reach room temperature before handling it. This recipe will make four crusts, each large enough to fit a 9-inch in diameter pie plate.

How to make a pie:

Spread a generous amount of flour on a large cutting board, clean counter or other surface large enough to accommodate rolling out one ball of dough. Roll out to desired size. Line the pie plate or other baking pan with the bottom crust. Do not stretch the crust over the pan or it will shrink during the baking process. Allow it to rest while you roll out the top crust. If you want to make a woven top crust, cut the strips now.

Pour the filling into the pastry-covered pan. Add the top crust. Trim outer edges and crimp them together with a fork or your fingers. Make slits in the top crust so steam built up during the baking process has escape vents. To prevent the outer edges of the crusts from burning, cover the edges with tinfoil. Some people glaze the top crust with milk or egg white and then dust with coarse sugar.

Follow the directions listed in a standardized cookbook for baking your variety of pie filling, whether it is
pumpkin, berry or custard. I often bake my pies at 350
degrees, sometimes less. If in doubt, check a recipe-tested
cookbook. Refrigerate any leftovers.

Suggestions for Adaptations to Specific Dietary Restrictions

When people gather at the family table these days, they often come with dietary restrictions. My husband is on a low-sodium diet, cannot have dairy products and has high cholesterol. One daughter does not consume foods containing gluten. Our daughter-in-law is a vegetarian, and our grandchildren tend to eat the same as their mother. All of us try to watch our caloric intake. Trying to compose meals compatible with everyone's needs at times puzzles me.

If you or your loved ones are in any of these situations, I hope the following suggestions help you adapt the recipes and adjust the ingredients of your heritage foods while maintaining the joy of eating. Perhaps you are already aware of how to omit/reduce ingredients and specific foods. Good for you! *Most important:* If you have not asked your loved one's primary care physician to refer him or her to a registered dietitian, do not delay. Often insurance policies will pay for one or two appointments with a dietitian, because she or he is the best way to begin this journey of modifying recipes and meals. In addition to the dietitian's assistance, I hope my suggestions, which follow, are helpful as well.

DAIRY-FREE

If a recipe includes milk, I substitute it with "milk" made from rice, soy or coconut. The end product, as in **Shirley's Baked Rice Custard**, will turn out different, so be prepared. It does not hurt to try the recipe in question at least once with the chosen milk substitute and see if it works for you. Water can often be used in place of milk, as in the recipe, **Lightning Quick Yeast Rolls.** Cheese? We have not found a decent substitute, but some lactose-insensitive people can eat goat's milk and cheese. With butter, leave it out. Use shortening, or try replacing the fat with olive oil. For recipes requiring oil, use a high-quality virgin olive oil. I find reducing the amount of oil and shortening by 2 tablespoons to 1/4 cup, depending on the recipe, cuts the calories and still turns' out an edible product. Sometimes I use solid coconut oil instead of shortening or butter, but you may not care for the flavor of coconut, and coconut oil is still a hydrogenated fat.

SODIUM/SALT

Omit all salt from the recipe! Your loved one's heart depends on it. Others can choose to season their food at the table. Herbs give main dish recipes added oomph. We use commercially prepared no-salt seasonings, and packaged no-salt mixes for chili, beef stew and tacos. Greatly reduce or omit baking powder and baking soda. Baking powder and baking soda are incredibly high in sodium (salt). If you do not believe me, take a look at the ingredients label on the back of a container of baking soda or baking powder, and then clutch your heart. My piecrust recipe does just fine without the full measure of these leavening agents, but you can kiss goodbye the recipe for dumplings. Leavening agents like baking soda or baking powder react with the addition of some type of moisture, and the application of heat during the cooking process to produce a gas. The gas expands the dough or batter so the finished product has volume or shape. The cookie recipes *may* work if you halve the amount of baking powder/soda. I have learned to work out a sodium-per-serving ratio. For instance, the recipe for **Pauline's Banana Bars**, with salt not included, calls for 1 teaspoon baking soda, which amounts to 1,200 milligrams of sodium for the entire batch. I bake the batter in a 9x13 pan then cut the baked bars into 20 rectangles. The result? Each piece contains 60 mg of added sodium. That amount is workable for someone on a sodium-restricted diet. Do not use self-rising flour. It contains sodium. Use low-sodium commercially produced products whenever possible, or make the whole thing from scratch as I suggested in the recipe for **Light in the Saddle Baked Beans.** For the recipe just mentioned, a person could use commercially canned no-salt-added tomatoes, but he or she may have to hunt to find them. Better yet, ask a supervisor at your local grocery store. Let him or her know you want to see low/no-sodium products on the shelves.

Note: Although a number of recipes featured in this book call for salt/baking soda/baking powder, as mentioned earlier, I either greatly reduce the amount called for, or eliminate the ingredient (like salt) altogether.

GLUTEN-FREE

I do not have a good hold on this one yet. There are lots of gluten-free recipes on the Internet but I followed the advice of our hospital's registered dietitian. Instead of trying to tinker with a bit of this special flour and that special ingredient, I hunted up a good company, Bob's Red Mill©, and purchased mixes from it. Bob's makes a good bread machine mix and the result is a decent loaf of bread. If the menu calls for rolls or hamburger buns, I stop the machine after the final stage of kneading and remove the dough. The dough is sticky, so I use a large spoon to scoop out the dough and then drop large blobs on a greased cookie sheet. I let the blobs rise and then bake them. It works, so the gluten-free folks in my family are happy. However, gluten-free mixes are quite high in salt/sodium.

Do not become discouraged. Learning to adapt favorite recipes is an ongoing process. When you do research, remember to snoop out good recipes from others in the same situation. As a person learns the craft of honoring special dietary needs, he or she will discover it is a journey with some success and some failure and ultimately rewarding because it keeps loved ones healthier and their eating as enjoyable as possible.

Bibliography

1) American Historical Society of Germans from Russia. "Kuche Kochen Cookbook." Lincoln, Nebraska, Eleventh Printing, 1982.

2) "Community Presbyterian Church Cookbook." Terry, Montana.

3) Johnson, Virginia Renoud. Personal Notes, 1990-99.

4) Montana State University. *MontGuide*s for *Rosa acicularis* Lindl, *Rosa arkansana* Porter, *Rosa nutkana* C. Presl, *Rosa woodsii* Lindl.

5) Oregon State University Archives. "Taste of the 'Chives, 2008: A Historical Recipe Showcase." 2008.

6) Raver, Anne. "New York Roses, Home to Root." "New York Times" 22 April 2009: D1.

7) Rudolf, Homer, ed. and Harold Ehrman. "The Glückstalers in New Russia, The Soviet Union, and North America." Glückstal Colonies Research Association, Richtman's Printing, Fargo, North Dakota. 2008. 83.

About the Author

Virginia A. Johnson, born in 1947, grew up in the northeast section of Portland, Oregon. She graduated from Oregon State University with bachelor's and master's degrees in home economics education and a bachelor's degree in elementary education.

Virginia taught students of all ages for a total of 16 years. She spent 12 of those years with elementary school children in the old Mill City-Gates School District.

Virginia is a freelance writer. She has more than 150 articles published in newspapers and periodicals. One of her fiction short stories, "Ornament of Grace", is featured in the anthology "Christmas in my Heart" (2012).

"A Greenhorn Gal: Life in Eastern Montana" is her first book-length work.

Virginia and her husband, Wayne, live most of the year in Crabtree, Oregon. Since 2001, they try to spend two months each year in Fallon, Montana, at their second home. The couple has three adult children and five grandchildren. To keep up with their extended family, the two shuttle between Oregon, Montana, California and Alaska on a regular basis.